*THE LAST SUPPER*

By the same author

**Stage Plays**
*Stripwell*
*Claw*
*The Love of a Good Man*
*Fair Slaughter*
*That Good Between Us*
*The Hang of the Gaol*
*The Loud Boy's Life*
*Birth on a Hard Shoulder*
*Crimes in Hot Countries*
*No End of Blame*
*Victory*
*The Power of the Dog*
*A Passion in Six Days*
*Downchild*
*The Castle*
*Women Beware Women* (with Thomas Middleton)
*The Possibilities*
*The Last Supper*
*The Europeans*
*The Bite of the Night*

**TV Plays**
*Cows*
*Mutinies*
*Prowling Offensive*
*Conrod*
*Heroes of Labour*
*Russia*
*Credentials of a Sympathizer*
*All Bleeding*
*Heaven*
*Pity in History*

**Radio Plays**
*One Afternoon on the 63rd Level of the North Face of the Pyramid of Cheops the Great*
*Henry V in Two Parts*
*Herman with Millie and Mick*
*Scenes from an Execution*

**Poetry**
*Don't Exaggerate; Desire and Abuse*
*The Breath of the Crowd*
*Gary the Thief/Gary Upright*

**Film**
*The Blow*

PLAYSCRIPT 114

# *THE LAST SUPPER:*
## *A New Testament*

Howard Barker

JOHN CALDER · LONDON
RIVERRUN PRESS · NEW YORK

First Published in Great Britain, 1988, by
John Calder (Publishers) Limited
18 Brewer Street, London W1R 4AS

and in the United States of America, 1988, by
Riverrun Press Inc.
1170 Broadway, New York, NY 10001

*British Library Cataloguing in Publication Data*

Barker, Howard
  *1946 –*   The last supper: a new testament.   (Playscript; v114)
  I. Title
  822 –.914
  ISBN 0-7145-4149-4

Typeset in 9/10pt Times by Artset (A division of Image Communications)
Printed in Great Britain by Hillman Printers (Frome) Ltd., Somerset

*For Ari Koskinen*
*of Helsinki*

## CHARACTERS

| | |
|---|---|
| LVOV | A Thinker |
| MARYA | A Nurse |
| ARNOLD | A Salesman |
| IVORY | An Aristocrat |
| SUSANNAH | A Cook |
| SLOMAN | A Carpenter |
| JUDITH | A Widow |
| GISELA | A Diaryist |
| DORA | A Teacher |
| ANNA | A Prostitute |
| FORJACKS | A Scholar |
| APOLLO | A Poet |
| ELLA | A Student |
| FIRST OFFICER | |
| SECOND OFFICER | |
| FARMER | |

## THE ACTORS OF THE PARABLES

| | |
|---|---|
| MacATTLEE | Soldiers |
| McSTAIN | " |
| McNOY | " |
| LITTLE MONK | |
| ABBOTT | |
| A FEMALE CHILD | |
| A WIDOW | |
| VIOLINIST | |
| NUN | |
| WOMAN LOOTER | |
| MALE DOCTOR | |
| A CHILD | |
| A WOMAN | |
| A GUNNER | |
| A SEAMSTRESS | |

THE CHORUS

## THE FIRST PROLOGUE

ELLA. We found God after all
Thinking He had disappeared
DORA. He had not disappeared
We found Him after all
Like the vagrant under the wall
He was only out of sight
ELLA. And He stood up in the light
Of all our shame and said
In the beam of our shame
Rubbed His eyes and said
DORA. I am not dead
I am the Public
ELLA. To me the heretics will
DORA. I am not dead
I am the Public
ELLA. And the transgressors
DORA. Genuflect
ELLA. The incurably deviant
DORA. Adore
ELLA. The breakers of vows
DORA. Applaud
ELLA. The habitually glum
DORA/ELLA. **Laugh you bastard, this is my creation, laugh.**
DORA. Did you think I'd died with religion?
Did you think I would succumb?
I have endured worse winters
Under the arches entertained the louse
ELLA. Quitting the cathedral in the night
DORA. God the Public needs no house
ELLA. And the sexually active bishops
DORA. The theologians with radio technique
ELLA. The fathers of gifted children
DORA. The rock musicians with castles
ELLA. The summer school students in states of undress
DORA. The carnival organizers
ELLA. The sweet-natured pickpockets
DORA. Shop stewards red-eyed in the billiard hall
ELLA. Popes and Mercenaries all
DORA. Concurred

ELLA. The Public
   We
   The Public
   We
   The Public
   Had to be God
DORA. Since God had to be
DORA/ELLA. **Applaud you bastards!**

*The terrible sound of laughter.*


### THE SECOND PROLOGUE

IVORY. I bring you an invitation
   Oh, no, she says, not an invitation
   Yes
   We are all so afraid
   Yes
   An invitation to hang up the
   **Suffocating overcoat of communication**
   Hang it up
   And those with biros write upon your wrist
   **The play contains no information**
   Aren't you tired of journalists?
   Oh, aren't you tired of journalists?
   No one will hold your hand tonight
   Nor oil you with humour
   As the swimmer is greased to pass through
   Water quicker
   No
   When the poem became easy it also became poor
   When art became mechanized it became an addiction
   I lecture!
   Oh, I lecture you! *(A terrible storm of laughter.)*
   Forgive!
   Forgive!

### THE PLAY

*A figure asleep in a hammock. An engine labouring. A* WOMAN *enters.*

MARYA. I'm still insane.
Obviously insane as ever. *(The train passes.)*
Goodbye you male scum! Goodbye you meat and gristle! *(She bares her breasts. A* MAN *enters, watches her. The wheels fade.)*

ARNOLD. You shout at all the trains. Your smear your breasts on all the windows. Goodbye you male scum! But how dedicated you are at the hospitals. Meeting the ambulance and wiping the broken bodies. Now, this is his influence. Isn't it? Your influence? *(The* FIGURE *is still.)* Pretend to be asleep. But I say it's your influence. **You have no desire to cure anybody.** Sleep on, sleep on. (IVORY *enters.)* **Cunt!**

IVORY. Let him sleep.

ARNOLD. Sleep? How can anyone sleep in the current state of things? We can only pretend, just as he is now pretending. He is fictive, aren't you? Fictive!

IVORY. We know he is fictive.

ARNOLD. We know it, but does he? Sleep is for times of stability. Even gardening has become impossible. Why do you say?

IVORY. No, I didn't say.

ARNOLD. Because it is absurd to plant what will never be allowed to flourish. I know you say plant anyway. Plant, and if it is trodden down, plant again. I have heard him say that.

MARYA. Plant, and even though armies trample fifty gardens one they will miss and there you may shelter.

ARNOLD. I have heard that —

IVORY. Often —

ARNOLD. Often I have heard that, but it is fictive, isn't it? Like all he says. **Wake up you utter cunt.** (THEY *look at* ARNOLD.) It so happens I require your fictiveness. **Cunt, wake up.** *(He stares at the hammock and its occupant. The sound of desolation fills the stage.)*

### THE FIRST PARABLE
#### The Irrepressible Optimism of the Demolition Squad

*Three* SOLDIERS *enter.*

ALL. We kill Nobody!

McSTAIN. They say civil wars are the worst but what's your evidence?

ALL. We kill Nobody!

MACATTLEE. They say it is terrible to lift your hand against your brother, but what's your evidence?

ALL. We kill Nobody!

McNOY. The Captain says the bell's our enemy. Seek out the churches, says our officer. He gave eight reasons for the unslinging of bells.

McSTAIN. The sound of four ton bells crashing to the belfry floor is one nobody expects to hear repeated in his lifetime.

McNOY. We did however, hear it repeated.

MACATTLEE. In fact, the sound, for all its uniqueness, became routine.

ALL. We kill Nobody!

MACATTLEE. We suffer from the dim awareness that these acts are having no significant impact on the outcome of the war.

McSTAIN. Certainly there are fewer bells.

McNOY. But equally certainly the fighting has grown worse.

ALL. We kill Nobody!

McNOY. We suffer from the dim awareness that the future will be worse than the past we swore to extinguish.

MACATTLEE. We imagine what it is to be happy. But what once made us happy no longer does.

McSTAIN. We are forced to conclude that happiness, if it exists at all, is continuing to do what we are doing *(A* MONK *enters.)*

LITTLE MONK. Welcome to the monastery! *(He bows.)*
    There is food and drink in the refectory.

MACATTLEE. Food and drink?

McSTAIN. What food?

MACATTLEE. What drink?

McNOY. In the middle of a war?

MACATTLEE. If it is the middle.

LITTLE MONK. Hot water. Towels.

McSTAIN. Hot water?

LITTLE MONK. In the prebendary.

ALL. **Old trick.**

McNOY. Ancient as the Greeks this insincere hospitality.

LITTLE MONK *(bowing).* I admit it. I am thinking not of your hunger, or of your thirst, but of the bells.

McSTAIN. The bells . . .

MACATTLEE. The bells again . . .

LITTLE MONK. I owe it to my soul to be sincere. I could not care if you were fed or starved. Now I suppose you will beat me, and I deserve to be beaten for not succeeding in loving you. *(He pulls up his habit, revealing his back.)* Beat me, then. But leave the bells. Beat me to death for my sins!

ALL. We kill Nobody . . .

LITTLE MONK. You do not kill? But beat? Surely you beat?

McSTAIN. We have, we have beaten, haven't we?

McNOY. I dimly recollect a beating, but that was far from here.

MACATTLEE. Not far from here. We have merely marched in circles.

McSTAIN. It was near, rather.

McNOY. Dim, dim, that memory . . .

LITTLE MONK *(scrambling to his feet)*. **Get away from here. You scum!**

MACATTLEE. You see, we must learn to keep our mouths shut.

LITTLE MONK. **Scum! I will thrash you with a branch!** *(He goes to kick* MACATTLEE, *who catches him by the foot.)*

McNOY. Tell us of the life of a monk.

LITTLE MONK *(shouting.)* Brothers! These soldiers do not kill!

McNOY. No, don't scream, tell us about the silent life.

LITTLE MONK. Monks! Monks!

*The* ABBOTT *enters.*

ABBOTT. Don't beat the little monk, I pray you.

McNOY. We leave the burning monasteries thinking, what kind of life was that?

ABBOTT *(kneeling.)* Beat me, if you must beat somebody.

LITTLE MONK. **They don't beat!**

ABBOTT. Soldiers who don't beat?

LITTLE MONK. Look!

McNOY. For example, the peace and quiet, does that stimulate the mind or deaden it?

ABBOTT. **Take their weapons!**

*The* LITTLE MONK *frees himself with a kick and seizes the rifles. He runs off with them.*

McSTAIN. You monks are all the same.

ABBOTT. Take yourselves to the crypt and lock the door!

McNOY. This could be paradise. Are you friendly with the nuns?

ABBOTT. If you return to your officers you will report the continued existence of the bells, and more soldiers will be sent, perhaps crueller than you. Obviously you must be locked away. Please co-operate. God loves the bells. We will free you when the war is over.

MACATTLEE. The war will not be over.

ABBOTT. We can pray.

MACATTLEE. You can pray, but it will not be over.

*The* LITTLE MONK *returns with a stick. He takes swipes at* McNOY.

LITTLE MONK. Sinners! I will confess this, obviously.

*Howard Barker*

ABBOTT. Restrain yourself.

LITTLE MONK. I can't help it!

ABBOTT. This is a foolish war. Everyone has forgotten why it started.

McSTAIN. That doesn't matter. It had a cause, that's the important thing. Now it exists for itself. It's the same with bells. The order to demolish has never been rescinded.

McNOY. Ow!

MacATTLEE. The officer who issued this order died in an air raid. We buried him in a town square near a fountain.

McSTAIN. Nish.

MacATTLEE. No, Pecs.

McSTAIN. Our memory fails us, but who wants a memory?

ABBOTT. Lie on the floor, or he will kick you. *(They lie down.)* Oh, God! I threatened them with violence and they acted!

LITTLE MONK. I want to beat them!

ABBOTT. No, no —

LITTLE MONK. **I want to beat them!**

ABBOTT *(turning away).* All right, beat them!

LITTLE MONK. Hey! *(He whacks their backs.)*

ABBOTT. We are beating our enemies . . .

LITTLE MONK. Now I want to kill them!

ABBOTT. No!

LITTLE MONK. Yes! *(He goes to thrash them again. The* ABBOTT *grabs him.)* Why not! Why not!

ABBOTT. I don't know, I only — *(They grapple with each other.)*

LITTLE MONK. Let me go!

ABBOTT. In the name of God, I —

LITTLE MONK. **I hate you! I hate you!** *(He slaps the* ABBOTT's *face. He stops. They are breathless.)* You see how we . . . you se how . . .

*A wind of desolation sweeps the stage.*

ABBOTT *(to the* SOLDIERS.*)* Go and take the bells down . . . go and . . . go and . . . *(The* SOLDIERS *get up, begin to work.)*

### END OF THE FIRST PARABLE

MARYA. Did you ever know anyone who slept so much?

IVORY. He stays up late.

MARYA. He stays up late, but did you ever know anyone who slept so much? I am offended by it. I regard it as an unfavourable comment on myself.

ARNOLD. On me, too.

MARYA. On all of us. As if what he dreamed were better than what we are.

IVORY. He dreams appalling truths.

MARYA. So what? I am a truth also. **A mad truth obviously.** I feel this need to kick him. Frequently I do.

ARNOLD. Kicks of love.

MARYA. Love kicks, yes.

ARNOLD. He knows this. He knows your kicks are compliments.

MARYA. That also is enraging. *(Sounds approaching.)* Another train! *(She exposes her breasts to a passing train.)* Goodbye you male scum! Goodbye you meat and gristle! *(It passes, fades. A* WOMAN *enters with a sack.)*

IVORY. Susannah, you are the absolute in dedication —

SUSANNAH. Shut up —

IVORY. The absolute in concentration —

SUSANNAH. **Shut up, will you!**

IVORY. Consideration, solicitation —

SUSANNAH *(flinging down the sack, which spill loaves all over the floor).* **Shut up, I said!**

MARYA. He means to compliment you.

SUSANNAH. He is ascribing tedious virtues to me. It's his way of belittling somebody.

ARNOLD. You can't say anything here . . .

SUSANNAH. If I don't do it, who will?

MARYA. Quite. Who will if you don't?

SUSANNAH. It is really so depressing, so enervating, that people like you who aviod every shred of responsibility or labour can demean the energy of others —

IVORY. I am not demeaning —

SUSANNAH. by applying sarcastic epithets to them such as —

IVORY. I abhor the charge —

SUSANNAH. trust or honesty or —

IVORY. Abhor! Abhor!

SUSANNAH. kindness in order to humiliate me! It is you who are humiliated! You! By idleness! By insolence! You! *(Pause.)*

ARNOLD. Extraordinary. Loaves! Extraordinary . . . *(He stares at them.)*

SUSANNAH. The carthorse thanked. The donkey praised. *(She turns to go.)* If you touch one crumb, I'll dislocate your spine. *(She goes.)*

ARNOLD. Poor Susannah.

MARYA. What's poor about her? It's you who's poor.

ARNOLD. Where does she get loaves from? At a time like this? It's extraordinary.

IVORY. She has a gift . . .

MARYA. You call everything a gift in order to spare yourself the tedium of imitating it.

IVORY. I am the object of contempt. I see.

MARYA. Yes.

IVORY. I am a thing of filth and disapprobation.

MARYA. You know you are.

IVORY *(walking out).* But there are worlds and worlds . . .

MARYA. You keep saying that. What does it mean? *(*IVORY *goes out.)* There are worlds and worlds, what does he mean?

ARNOLD. I think it's something he got from Lvov. *(He kneels. Begins to stack the loaves. Suddenly he stops.)* He gets furious if you wake him. *(Pause.)* Well, I say furious. I mean, there is a certain expression of — resentment — in his face. Probably he is dreaming of something of enormous significance. Probably he is in torment. *(He peers at the SLEEPING MAN.)* And his lips move, his lips go, and his brows are all, I say to him, you don't know the meaning of peace! To which he says —

*A* CHORUS *of figures has appeared.*

CHORUS. **He's dreaming us again.**
ARNOLD. Peace?
CHORUS. **Us.**
ARNOLD. Peace? *(He laughs.)*
CHORUS. **Us the father and the mother.**
ARNOLD. Peace!
CHORUS. **Unanimity and solidarity**
 **Community and family**
 **Us**
 **He's dreaming us again**
 **The crowd is also a divinity**
 **He's dreaming our**
 **Revenge.**

*Pause.*

LVOV. What are you afraid of?
ARNOLD. I don't know . . .
LVOV. You are always afraid of something. **What?**
ARNOLD. I don't know, I don't know . . . *(He starts stacking loaves.)*
LVOV. **Then why are you trembling?** *(*ARNOLD *shakes his head.)* It's no wonder I sleep so much, it is the only refuge from your misery. **I also am finite.**
ARNOLD. Of course . . .
LVOV. Pity is not bottomless. It is not a well, is it?
ARNOLD. No, indeed . . .
LVOV. Not a well at all. In my case, it is more like a saucer. Shallow. Simply spilled. Woops! Mine's spilled! No pity left! Where's everybody?
MARYA. Every day you say that. Every time you wake up. Where's everybody? Do you think we just sit about waiting for you to —
LVOV. Yes. *(Pause.)*
MARYA. Yes, it's true. *(She shrugs.)* It's true! When you are asleep we merely quarrel.
ARNOLD. There is no mutton to be had. No fowl. No fish. Nothing.
MARYA. How do you know?
ARNOLD. Sloman says.
MARYA. Sloman says? Why don't you look? Sloman says!

ARNOLD. **You thrust your tits at trains all day and then tell me to look for mutton I hate your tits you look.** *(Pause.)*

MARYA. You see? We quarrel even when you are awake. *(To* ARNOLD.*) There is food. There is always food. It conceals itself, that's all.*

*An* OFFICER *enters.*

OFFICER. Lvov? *(Pause.)* Which one of you's —

ARNOLD. He is Lvov. *(Pause. The* OFFICER *goes towards* LVOV.*)* **Don't kill him.** *(The* OFFICER *looks at* ARNOLD, *confused. Pause.)* So much — so much — killing . . . *(He sits on a stool, shrunkenly.* MARYA *goes to him, nurses his head.)*

OFFICER *(to* LVOV*).* My train leaves in an hour. Are you Lvov? My train leaves in an hour. *(Pause.)* **Well, tell me what to do, then!** *(Pause. He tears off his cap and sits earnestly on a chair.)* It is so very easy to repeat the argument that life should not be taken. I have read the argument and it convinced me every time. And yet I never was convinced. How could I have been because I — *(Pause.)* **Well, are you Lvov or not?** *(Pause. He snatches up his cap and leaves, as* SLOMAN *enters, holding a sack.)*

SLOMAN *(holding out the sack).* Mutton, no. But bitch! Not a very healthy bitch, because the healthy dogs were either nimble, and evaded capture, or if not nimble, then already stewed and a figment in the alimentary memory. Consequently, only she who looked fatal to digest could be lured to my sack. Once in the sack I — *(Pause.)* It is terribly hard to kill a dog. I suffered. Will against horror. Will and more will. *(Pause.)* It is quite right that I who loved dogs should have been sent. Quite right. Am I to skin it also? *(*LVOV *ignores him.)* Silly question. *(He turns to go, then abruptly flings the sack at* LVOV, *who catches it.)* **You skin it.** *(Pause.)* If this is to be our final dinner I think you should do some of the preparation. Seven years I have known you and never once **I sound like a housewife on the edge of mutiny** not once have you. So you. *(Pause.* LVOV *is still.)* He looks so —

He has his expression of —

**Are you catching his expression?**

ARNOLD. Shut up, Sloman . . .

SLOMAN. His pained and injured — like a bruise burst open expression — I have grown utterly to hate . . . *(Pause.)* Still, we have, all of us, only a limited repertoire of expression. I accept — barring the effect of gunfire on the physiognomy — barring traumatic wounding — this is an expression we shall have to live with. And there's the knife. *(He chucks a blade to* LVOV. *It falls to the floor.)* I never felt so strongly in my life — never more — democratic. *(He looks to* MARYA.*)* Oh, say you know what I mean! *(Pause. He picks up the blade and takes the sack from* LVOV.*)* I'll skin it obviously. *(He goes out.)*

LVOV. You announce the last supper and they don't hurry themselves, do they?

MARYA. They are all over the continent and there is a war on —

LVOV. They don't hurry themselves. They tidy their beds. They nail soles on their boots. They linger in bookshops in old cities. Don't they believe me any more?

ARNOLD. There is a war on, Lvov —

LVOV. I say this is the last supper and two, as usual, do all the work.

ARNOLD. I would do more, but —

LVOV. The two who do the work perhaps do it because they love me more. Or perhaps they do it because work is a habit, and it comes easily to them. I don't praise them for it.

MARYA. I would do more as well, but —

LVOV. I'm not asking for excuses —

MARYA. I'm not excusing myself, I want to explain —

LVOV. I am bored with explanations —

MARYA. I am a boring woman but bores must be indulged or fascination could not know itself —

LVOV. You quote me —

MARYA. All the time —

LVOV. With failing conviction —

MARYA. Possibly —

LVOV. Routinely —

MARYA. Possibly — no, not at all — you —

ARNOLD. I met him on a road between the coast and the silted harbour, and I said, even at twenty yards I said, there is no other man like this. From his features alone, I knew there was no other.

MARYA. That must be true of any face.

ARNOLD. Obviously.

MARYA. Since all faces are different.

ARNOLD. Obviously

MARYA. We are an infinite variety.

ARNOLD. Any fool knows that. You are so trite for a lunatic. Any fool knows that. But his face. It was a face of extraordinary originality. Both coarse and refined. Even the passage of a cloud across the sun could bring out one, or other, aspect . . .

MARYA. It's true of any face —

ARNOLD. **You are so mercilessly trite.** Why be insane if you merely repeat slogans? What is the virtue in it? *(Pause.)*

MARYA. Why were you on the road?

ARNOLD. I was always on the road, wasn't I, Lvov? Always on the road?

SUSANNAH *enters with a sack, she tips out a pile of potatoes.*

ARNOLD. My God, my God, Susannah . . .

SUSANNAH. Will. And more will! *(She smiles triumphantly.)* Do you hate me, Lvov? I do it for you, and your face is. Your frown is. A reproving ditch across your brow. *(She looks at him, closely.)* Never mind. I do it for you. I would have taken these from the groping hands of blinded babies. And still it would be for you. *(Pause.)* As it was I —

MARYA. **She stole them from the orphanage!**

SUSANNAH *(not moving)*. Speak, then, Lvov . . .
MARYA. She stole them from the orphanage!
SUSANNAH. Speak then, you appalling man . . . *(Pause.)*
LVOV. They are very fine potatoes.
SUSANNAH. No, thank me.
MARYA. Anyone could steal them!
SUSANNAH *(turning on her)*. Could they? Can you imagine the will I
    found for that? My conscience I smothered with both hands. **Thank me
    you appalling man.** *(Pause.)* He won't, will he?
LVOV. If you love me, should I be surprised you break with trivial cons-
    cience? That is the essence of love. But I kiss you anyway. Stealing from
    the rich is facile but — *(He dries, shudders.)*
ARNOLD. Train!

*A fast train approaches.* LVOV *suddenly grabs* SUSANNAH, *shuddering.
She looks at him, appalled.* MARYA *opens her gown to the train, then closes
it again. The train goes.*

MARYA. Guns . . .
ARNOLD. What's wrong with guns? Why not expose your tits to guns? A
    gun might blush, I daresay. A gun might suffer.
MARYA. You try to sound like Lvov, but all you do is make a fool of yourself.
    You think you are poetic but you are simply absurd.
ARNOLD. The absurd may be poetic.
MARYA. When I was in the hospital the doctors said, paint! Paint your feel-
    ings! Write! Write your feelings! I didn't want to. What do they think art
    is? Vomit?
ARNOLD. Art is sometimes vomit.
MARYA. How would you know! You are a travelling salesman.
ARNOLD. I know what it is to vomit —
LVOV *(freeing himself from* SUSANNAH*)*. Stop . . . do stop . . . this tide
    of wit and banter, stop . . . stop . . . When I'm gone you'll simply —
ARNOLD. Gone? Gone where?
LVOV. Simply degenerate into wit and banter.
ARNOLD. Gone where?
LVOV. Sit at the road side gibbering . . .

*An immaculately dressed* WOMAN *enters.*

JUDITH. They have hanged some soldiers. *(She takes off her gloves.)* Quite
    rightly. *(She looks around.)* Am I early? The soldiers wanted to go home.
    No, said the officers, the war's not over, how can you go home? *(She looks
    around again.)* No tables? No chairs? Still, we want to go home say the
    soldiers in various illiterate tongues. This is supposed to be some sort of
    occasion, isn't it and I've — well, I always dress like this but — may I have
    a chair? *(*ARNOLD *brings her a chair. She sits.)* What perfect potatoes!
    I never thought to see potatoes so — inflexibly potato-like again — who
    — *(She quickly kneels, picks one up.)* May I keep this? To plant? *(She sits*

again.) You see, I believe in the future. *(She pops it in her bag.)* But they
are like heffers! They have a notion of home, and wild with home-sickness
they charge the barrack gates! Heads! Yes, heads against the solid planks,
boom! Boom! And blood! That is how mad they are! All this is well
enough, this is just the crazed instinct of males, much applauded in battle
and tolerated in the public bar but then . . . *(Pause.)* One less, or more
crazed than the others, pulls from his pocket a handkerchief-sized, flimsy
and scarcely-recognizable emblem called — a flag. But not the legal flag.
This particular combination of colours means — this pattern has —
resonances and — hieroglyphic significances which — its mere
appearance is enough to — **and up go the gallows!** Tree trunks, one across
the other, most crude carpentry, the bark is still on — and they dangle two
from either end, the homesick soldiers are suspended like pheasants from
a butcher's hook — do you remember pheasants? And make an avenue
down which — *(Pause.)* They say of me, Judith will never be without
stockings if the war reduces the rest of us to nakedness. It appears I am a
witch, but I merely read newspapers, and I thought ten years ago, stockings will cease, perhaps for all time, so I went from draper to draper, clearing them out. Admittedly, there is something absurd about them now . . .
*(She strokes her knee.)* Lvov says, you are afraid of something, or you
wouldn't dress so well, don't you, Lvov? Yes, I am afraid. I am afraid of
Lvov. And he is vain, God knows, his simplicity is so orchestrated. At least
I'm honest. **Ha! I hate that phrase!** *(She takes the potato from her bag.)*
Can't wait. *(She bites into it.)* By the way I'm widowed. *(They look at her.*
MARYA *goes to comfort her.)* No, don't touch! *(She shuts her eyes.)*
Don't mutter or console . . . ! *(Pause.)*

LVOV. How like you to announce this in such a calculated way. How
insincere.

JUDITH. Yes.

LVOV. To make a work of art of it.

JUDITH. Yes. You taught me that. You taught me information is nothing,
and expression, all. You are the actor, and me, the scene shifter, learning
from the wings . . .

ARNOLD. We are sorry. Notwithstanding you hate sentiment. I must tell
you I am moved for you.

MARYA. **Why doesn't she just let us give!** *(*SLOMAN *enters with a server
and lid.)*

SLOMAN. One joint of bitch.

MARYA. You must give. You will decay inside if you don't give.

SLOMAN. **One joint of bitch!** *(He whisks off the lid, replaces it with a
flourish.)*

MARYA. You will atrophy and stink. Your guts will rattle in your concave
belly like string in a paper bag.

ARNOLD. Judith's husband is dead.

MARYA. **It's true what I'm telling you!** *(*SLOMAN *shrugs.)*

JUDITH. There are many advantages in this. For one thing, he is not
maimed. I could not have born the return of damaged goods. You have

seen them, and so have I, and I always said to him, don't return like that,
I have neither the pity nor the responsibility for it.

ARNOLD. You have the pity.

JUDITH. All right, yes, I have the pity, but the pity would destroy my life.
*(She gets up.)* Perhaps he lay out in some wood somewhere, horribly hurt,
and thinking of me, put a bullet in himself. Do you think that's possible?

MARYA. Very possible.

JUDITH. They do that. They do do that, don't they?

LVOV. He would have lay sick in a room, and you would have ignored him.

JUDITH. Yes.

LVOV. His eyes would follow you round the room.

JUDITH. If he had eyes.

LVOV. If he had eyes, yes. And they would be a lake of misery, knowing you
were coming here.

JUDITH. Yes. And you would not give me one hour more. Not yield one
minute for his needs.

LVOV. Not one. *(Pause.)*

JUDITH. So, all this is good. All this is proper.

SLOMAN. It is not Lvov's way, is it, to let the weak distract the strong? Lvov
surrenders nothing.

LVOV. Would you be here if I did? If I were naked, would you admire me?
Because I have clothing, and there are many without. If I were filthy,
would you admire me? For there are those without soap, and I keep soap.
If I were all day carrying the crippled to the well, would you admire me?
Because there are many without water, and I have strength. I am what I
am and cannot be consumed in charity.

SLOMAN. No, nor in skinning dogs. Nor gathering potatoes. Or clearing
drains when the drains are blocked.

IVORY *(entering).* **Shut up you worthless shut up I hate your shut up you
drain cleaner.** *(He shudders, ceases. Pause. He goes to* JUDITH *and
embraces her.)*

LVOV *(to* SLOMAN*).* You understand, while pretending not to. You make
a rattle of democracy, while knowing how much better it is you cook than
me. You see, and you deny. You have never ceased resenting, and when the
truth stands out like a swollen vein, you resent that, too. Resent the stars
if you wish. Or the fact that water runs downhill.

SLOMAN. No. *(He shakes his head.)*

No.

No.

This is an odd time for an argument, but the best arguments break out at
odd times. You are ascribing my democracy to a flaw in my character —

JUDITH. Your nature is flawed —

SLOMAN. My nature is neither here nor there —

IVORY. **Put the dog down —**

SLOMAN. You are obsessed with Lvov, all of you, and you interpret all he
says in the light of truth, you will not see it when he trowels on spurious
arguments, the more spurious he is the more you call it inspiration —

LVOV. **The dog you bastard the dog —**

SLOMAN. There is no flaw in my nature which is not also in his —

ARNOLD. You are spilling the dog —

SLOMAN. And what if I do ram my head against the trees? What if I do? Perhaps I hate the universe. Perhaps I wish water would run uphill. And if democracy is as hard as scooping the stars out of the sky, so what, the effort is good, the effort is admirable —

JUDITH. It is not admirable, it is futile and ridiculous —

SLOMAN. Seven years I have listened to his arguments and I feel like saying —

IVORY. **Drop the dog and I will bite your lungs out.** *(Pause. He laughs.)* No, it's true, it's true, we are all incapable of discernment. It's perfectly true what he says we are infatuated. It's perfectly true we have allowed ourselves to be. It's perfectly true the power of Lvov resides solely in his refusal to apologize. Perfectly, perfectly true and I for one refuse to. I for one. *(Pause.)*

SLOMAN *(to* JUDITH*).* I'm sorry, I — I shouldn't have — when your husband is —

JUDITH. That is all absorbed. It lives only in the marrow now. Blind sediment.

SLOMAN. That may be so, but —

JUDITH. It is so. *(*SLOMAN *goes out with the tray.)*

MARYA. Judith, you will live for such a long, long time.

JUDITH. Why do you say that?

MARYA. Because you are unloving. Unhating. But unloving too. I think you will live to be hundreds!

LVOV. She does love. It is knowledge she loves.

JUDITH. Yes! When the telegram arrived I was more interested in how I would react than I was in the information itself. For months I had prepared myself, and immediately I threw all his things in two large boxes, and sent the boxes to his mother.

LVOV. That was good. The things will help his mother to die, whereas they would only have prevented your living. *(Pause. She absorbs this.)*

JUDITH. Lvov knows . . . ! Lvov has never loved anyone, but he knows! When I was a girl I hunted men who knew things, who had done things. My husband, for example, had been a cowboy in Argentina! Yes, I never told you, but he had, and at fifteen had been a stowaway to the East Indies! What he didn't know! But Lvov, who lived all his life in one place, Lvov knows more, don't you, Lvov? Will you teach us something new tonight? I must know something new . . . *(The sound of desolation.)*

## THE SECOND PARABLE
### *The Ashamed and the Unashamed*

*A* CHILD *enters. She looks around her. She lets out a cry.*

CHILD. Help!
  Help!

*(Pause. An* OLD WOMAN *appears.)*

WIDOW. Why should anyone help you?

CHILD. Because one day I'll be powerful and anyone who didn't help me will be made to suffer.

WIDOW. I'm suffering already and anyway you won't live to be adult. Someone will murder you and hide you in a ditch.

CHILD. How can you tell?

WIDOW. Your mouth.

CHILD. What about it?

WIDOW. Says murder me.

CHILD. Give us a room.

WIDOW. No rooms.

CHILD. **Got a big house.**

WIDOW. Pigs in all the rooms.

CHILD. Pigs . . . ?

WIDOW. Yes, you know pigs, they eat the dead.

CHILD. Turn a pig out.

WIDOW. For you? There's a war on.

CHILD. Always been a war on. As long as I can remember.

WIDOW. Me too.

CHILD. I'll die of cold.

WIDOW. No, you won't, you'll be murdered.

CHILD. I am one of a million homeless children, so I read.

WIDOW. I am one of a million miserable widows, so I heard.

CHILD. **It's snowing.**

WIDOW *(turning to go in).* Thank God the pigs are dry.

CHILD. I'm not ashamed of being poor. I'm not ashamed of being homeless. I'm not ashamed of stealing. Nor of kicking old men when they're down.

WIDOW. No one is ashamed of anything any more. For example, I am not ashamed of having seven rooms. I am not ashamed of eating pork. I am not ashamed of leaving children in the snow. This is the effect of unending war. Now clear off. I hate vagrants even more than they hate me. *(She turns again.)*

CHILD. Just a minute! *(She stops.)* One of us could try to be ashamed. If you like, I will. *(Pause.)*

WIDOW. You don't look it. It's that mouth again.

CHILD. I don't know what ashamed looks like.

WIDOW. If I remember, it was sort of — I can't do it either —

CHILD. We can't do it because we don't feel it . . .

WIDOW. The snow's so deep I shan't get back to the house!

CHILD. Now you look ashamed! That's it!

WIDOW. It's not shame, I'm frightened — *(She starts to go out, painfully.)*

CHILD. I'll get to the house before you! I'll shut the door and you can die to the sound of pig slaughtering!

WIDOW. Do you think that'll stop you being murdered? *(The* CHILD *stops.)* Delay it, that's all.

CHILD. That's all I ask. Delay and more delay. *(Pause.)*
Now I can't see the house! Which way to the house?

WIDOW. Not telling.

CHILD. We'll drown in the snow!

WIDOW. I always thought I'd die alone, but no, it turns out differently . . .

CHILD. I can't move!

WIDOW. It was always like this in December . . .

*(Three figures appear, muffled, in the distance.)*

CHILD. Look! People!

WIDOW. Don't call them!

CHILD. I must!

WIDOW. If you call them, you'll only regret it.

CHILD. If I don't call them I'll regret it!

WIDOW. There are worse things than dying.

CHILD. **Help! Help!**

WIDOW. Idiot.

CHILD. They're waving!

WIDOW. Idiot. Idiot.

*The* THREE SOLDIERS *appear.*

McNOY. We're coming!

McSTAIN. We see you!

MacATTLEE. We kill nobody! *(They pick their way over the stage.)*

WIDOW. You had to call help. Now look at us. If I had taken no notice how perfect everything would have been. I know I should never have left the house. One error! That's all it takes! One error and every error follows after! This comes of heeding the human voice.

ALL SOLDIERS *(looking)*. Women in holes . . .

WIDOW. Only pigs are worth replying to.

ALL SOLDIERS. **Pigs! Where?**

WIDOW. You see, everything's the result of everything else!

ALL SOLDIERS. **What pigs?**

CHILD. On the bed.

MacATTLEE. On the bed?

CHILD. In the bathroom.

McNOY. In the bathroom?

WIDOW. Kill everything. Kill the lot!

McSTAIN. To think we might have just passed by!

McNOY. We did pass by.

McSTAIN. When?

McNOY. Often. There is the house with the filthy shutters.

MacATTLEE. I dimly remember a house with shutters but that was far from here.

McNOY. Not far from here. We have merely marched in circles.

McSTAIN. My memory fails me, but who wants a memory? *(They make towards the house.)*

CHILD. Don't just go!

MacATTLEE. We thought you were hiding, but you fell in. It is always hard to tell why people are in holes. *(He extends a hand to help her. She takes it.)* What a wonderful mouth you have got . . . *(The CHILD looks to the WIDOW apprehensively.)* No, I think I will stay in the hole.

MacATTLEE. Please yourself. *(He walks towards the house.)*

WIDOW. What about me!

McSTAIN. What about you?

WIDOW. Get me out!

McSTAIN. Get out yourself. *(He walks away. Pause.)*

CHILD. My mouth could have got me out. My mouth was a rope. Whereas your mouth, pinched purse of a thing, keeps you in . . .

WIDOW. I tell you, when they have eaten the pigs, God help us.

CHILD. Why?

WIDOW. You know what happens when men have eaten.

CHILD. No, what happens?

WIDOW. They want love.

CHILD. **Love?**

WIDOW. Unfortunately, yes. I experienced a great deal of love when the war and I were still young . . . *(Pig squeals offstage.)*

CHILD. Does it hurt?

WIDOW. Frequently, it's fatal.

CHILD. Smell that!

WIDOW. Pig fat. Our hour draws nearer. Our calvary.

CHILD. If the sun would shine, the snow would melt . . .

WIDOW. What do you call that? Wisdom? *(Singing offstage.)*

CHILD. They should be ashamed . . .

WIDOW. I will suggest it to them. Because while we aren't ashamed, if they were, all would be well!

*The* SOLDIERS *appear, smiling and lurching. They come to the rim of the holes.* McNOY's *hand reaches out to the child.)*

WIDOW. You should be ashamed! Have you nothing better to do? *(*McNOY *nudges* MacATTLEE. MacATTLEE *reaches out to the* WIDOW.)* Pinched purse or not. Now you see that loveliness has nothing to do with anything.

McSTAIN. They keep their haunches under the snow. So warm, the haunches . . .

ALL SOLDIERS. **We kill no — body**

*Pause. The hands are outstretched. At last the* WOMEN *concede, put out their hands. At the moment the hands touch, a distant sound seeps over the stage. The* SOLDIERS *listen, caught. It is the sound of bells.* MCSTAIN *drifts under their spell, offstage.* MCNOY *and* MACATTLEE *are unable to move.*

### END OF THE SECOND PARABLE

TWO WOMEN *enter in coats.*

GISELA *(putting down a bag).* Things are getting worse. Or is that a superficial judgement?

DORA. They are not getting worse. They are merely becoming different.

GISELA. That's not a bit superficial! *(She opens her arms, looking at* LVOV. *Then she goes to him and kisses him.)* Mmmm!

JUDITH. Why do you always go mmmmm when you kiss someone? What is the mmmmm meant to imply?

DORA. We all have habits.

JUDITH. It is so false. It means, if it means anything at all, that you feel it should be a pleasure and it isn't. Is that what it means? If it is a pleasure go mmmmm and mean it, if it isn't, shut up.

DORA. We all have habits.

JUDITH. So you said.

DORA. And that is her habit.

JUDITH. Well, smash it. Do you desire Lvov? Of course you do. Then say so!

GISELA *(turning to* JUDITH.*)* You look more beautiful than you have ever looked. *(*LVOV *bursts out laughing.)* She does! That was not a tactic! She does!

JUDITH. Yes. I am impeccably got up. Got up to the zenith!

IVORY. Underneath, a dog's dinner. But done up to the zenith!

DORA. She is not a dog's dinner.

JUDITH. When did you last see me?

DORA. In the flesh? Never.

JUDITH. Well, allow me to judge. I am beautifully packed.

GISELA. We have only just arrived and already we are busily flattering Judith. That is how quickly we slip into old habits, wars or no wars. Lvov, if everyone arrives tonight, it will be a miracle.

DORA. The roads are rivers, so to avoid the roads they drive on the fields, and then the fields become rivers. The abuse! The sullen style of abuse! Even the language is dying. We are coming to the end.

MARYA. The end of what? What is coming to an end? The war?

DORA. Complexity. We are witnessing the death of complexity.

MARYA. Oh, that. Well, good.

DORA. You would say so. It horrified you.

MARYA. It drove me mad.

DORA. It drove you mad, but for me, it was the whole point of existence. I was teaching a class in the city, a class which dwindles week by week, and today, no one appeared at all. So I stood at the front and lectured, and I was more articulate than at any other time of my life.

ARNOLD. It seemed so to you. But who was there to judge?

DORA. Everything I said was true. Everything, perfectly expressed.

GISELA *(taking off her coat)*. It's true, I do desire Lvov. I desire him, and he knows it. Why pretend I don't? But it's complex. Sometimes I desire him, and sometimes I don't. I think that is what I mean when I go mmm. *(DORA laughs and hugs GISELA.)*

MARYA. Who cares what you mean? I don't. *(LVOV moves to the front of the stage. The sound of a murmuring crowd rises.)*

LVOV. I don't want to come! I don't want to come! *(The sound is swamped by a mass of laughter.)* Of course they are absurd! I see they are absurd, and the more absurd they are the less I want to leave them, why! *(A mass of laughter.)*

CHORUS. **The masses**
**The masses**
**They sing so beautifully**
**The masses**
**They tear the flags from gates**
**And the eagles from the thrones of governors**
**And piss into the mouths of dying officers!**

*The sound of a train.*

ARNOLD. Ambulance train! Marya! They let one through!

MARYA. Oh, look at the length of it!

ARNOLD. Ambulance train! *(MARYA ties a scarf round her head and hurries out. At last the train passes. Fades.)* Normally they let them rot in sidings.

JUDITH. The army of the living must take precedence. I should have thought that was obvious.

ARNOLD. Dying in the sidings . . .

JUDITH. **They don't die in the sidings! That is so — that is so utterly —** *(Pause.)* What is the use of these emotional expressions —

IVORY. Their breath is like a wind which whistles down the corridors —

JUDITH. If they are not true? That surely is the rot of poetry?

LVOV. The posturing of pity obscures —

JUDITH. Yes, and nothing comes of it but sex. Sex and more sex!

DORA. You interrupted him. You interrupted Lvov.

JUDITH. Did I?

DORA. No one lets Lvov finish any more.

JUDITH. I'm sorry. I'm sorry, Lvov. *(Pause.)*

ARNOLD. She is tense. She is tense because —

JUDITH. I'm not. *(Pause.)* I apologize, but actually I think I could have finished it for him. He was going to say, obscures the secret pleasure in another's agony. Is that right?

LVOV. Yes. *(The mass of laughter passes.)* Yes, I was . . . *(Pause, painful.)*

GISELA. It's obvious that anyone who has been taught as long as we have will know the method of the teacher. I see nothing very significant in our being able, after so long, to parody or imitate Lvov. It is perhaps, a sign of his greatness . . .

DORA. I think Gisela is aware, and possibly afraid, she could surpass Lvov . . .

GISELA. In Lvovness! In the elaboration of Lvov!

DORA. Yes . . . *(A further painful pause. The door opens with a flourish.)*

ANNA. Gin! Gin, bitches! *(She chucks the bottle at* DORA, *who catches it, laughing.* LVOV *goes to* ANNA *and embraces her again and again, silently, desperately.)*

ARNOLD. No one here drinks gin . . .

ANNA. Learn! It was a present from the last fat man in Europe!

JUDITH. Fresh from the brothel.

ANNA. Soldiers' stench in every pore and a slippery arse!

JUDITH. No time to wash —

ANNA. No time at all —

JUDITH. Towel between the legs and —

ANNA. Money in the handbag! *(They both laugh. They embrace.)*

LVOV. Anna, you will bury us all.

ANNA. Not deep, Lvov . . .

LVOV. Not deep, no.

ANNA. No time for deep graves.

JUDITH. Prick in one hand, shovel in the other . . .

DORA. It isn't true that Anna will survive. Lvov wants to believe it. It is pure Lvov to want the whore to birth the future, but it isn't true, she will be strangled in a dirty room . . .

ANNA. Dora, you refuse all hope . . . !

DORA. Yes . . .

ANNA. I love you. How you refuse! Worthless hope!

DORA. I do. I do refuse. Kiss me! *(They kiss, fondly.)*

GISELA. Lvov thinks corruption runs off Anna, like rain off an apple. We all have to believe in Anna's essential cleanliness. It is mandatory.

ANNA. Mandatory yes! What does that mean?

GISELA. You know perfectly well.

ANNA. I wish I was literate.

DORA. You are literate.

ANNA. I wish I was numerate.

DORA. You count money, don't you, at the door?

ANNA. I wish I was wicked!

JUDITH. You are wicked. What you mean is sinful, and sinful you will never be. A thousand men might lie on you, lathering, and you could skip up and your taste would all be honeyed. It's true isn't it? She is like that. She sweats purity. What do you say, Lvov? You are passionate about Anna. *(Pause.)*

LVOV. I think it is easy to love a prostitute. But because it is easy, it is not less worthy. I love Anna for her self. But I also love you, who is not yourself. It is only Dora I find hard to love. *(Pause.)*

DORA. I'm glad. *(ANNA laughs loudly.)* **It's true. I'm glad.**

ANNA. I believe you!

JUDITH. Lvov did not answer my question, did you, Lvov?

ARNOLD. It's his method.

DORA. It's his method, yes.

GISELA. His method is to counter questions with a statement generally related to the theme but —

ANNA. Leave him alone, you cows . . .

DORA. That's true, gradually you discover what defines Lvov, and it's deflection. Skilful, I admit.

JUDITH. I asked if Anna could be sinful —

ANNA. I fucking can —

DORA. Fucking has nothing to do with it —

ANNA. You are such a bony cow.

GISELA. Shh —

ANNA. You stand there like a bony cow and —

LVOV. Shh —

ANNA. No, she is, she is, isn't she, Arnold, a bony cow? *(He looks up from a chair.)* **Arnold!** *(She goes to him, puts her arms round his neck.)* No, don't finger me! You say hello to Arnold and immediately he —

ARNOLD. That's not so! That's so unfair! That's not so!

IVORY. It is so.

ARNOLD. I resent that!

IVORY. It is so. It is in your nature.

LVOV. Let him finger you, if fingering is what he wants.

ARNOLD. Good God, if you can't put your — good God! *(ANNA laughs.)*

SLOMAN *(who has entered and watched this).* This is what I mean by equality.

ARNOLD *(to LVOV).* You give me permission — you condescend to — license me to — *(He shakes his head with anger.)*

SLOMAN. This is what I mean when I talk of equality. There is none. This is what gets you in the end. The gnawing, humiliating absence of equality.

GISELA. What is humiliating about the absence of equality? Where is the humiliation in acknowledging another's qualities? His superiority even? Oh, God, what's humiliating in that? *(Pause. SLOMAN looks at him.)*

SLOMAN. It gnaws. *(Pause.)* It gnaws you even . . .

JUDITH. The ugly against the beautiful. The blind against the sighted.

SLOMAN. Yes.

JUDITH. The gnawing sense you lack blue eyes.

SLOMAN. I didn't say anything could be achieved. I said it gnaws. But Arnold cannot touch Anna, and Lvov can. It gnaws.

ARNOLD. No, I'm all right, I —

SLOMAN. Oh, Arnold, be gnawed! *(Pause.)* I also find Lvov — immaculate. I too, stoop to Lvov. And Susannah — *(She enters with a tray.)*

— she carries **every fucking thing** — *(ANNA goes to assist SUSAN-NAH.)* No! *(ANNA stops.)* But Lvov would no more take her in his arms than he would — fornicate with a prolapsed mare . . . *(Pause.)*

GISELA. We come together and —

We come together for —

Lvov . . . ! *(He is not observing them.)*

SLOMAN. I must — in the interests of clarity and truth — which was the first condition of our unity — speak what is to me at least — blindingly self-evident — but unperceived by you — which is that —

LVOV. You wish me to be inhuman. *(Pause.)*

SLOMAN. Yes. Obviously.

LVOV. I am perfectly human. And the perfectly human is as near to in-humanity as you should want. If I have power over Anna, you should be glad.

SLOMAN. Yes, but —

LVOV. You are angry that you are not me. Your body and your soul are raw, as if you were inverted and your red insides were smarting in the air.

SLOMAN. I can't reply to that —

LVOV. It is the terrible cry of the skinned wolf whose nostrils are brimming with its own blood . . .

SLOMAN. I can't reply. I would rather help Susannah —

LVOV. You are not helping Susannah, you are using her. You are using her against me. *(Pause.)*

SLOMAN. Yes . . . *(Pause. He gathers himself, goes to leave the room. As he does so, a FARMER enters, taking off his cap.)*

FARMER. Are you Lvov?

SLOMAN. I'm not Lvov. *(He goes out. The FARMER goes to ARNOLD.)*

FARMER. Are you Lvov? *(ARNOLD shakes his head. The FARMER goes to IVORY.)* I have a problem. *(JUDITH laughs. The FARMER turns to leave.)*

GISELA. Don't go. It doesn't hurt to be laughed at. What you said was funny, whether you knew it or not. *(Pause.)*

FARMER. She sits there in her — *(He shrugs.)* She sits and — *(He shrugs.)*

GISELA. It doesn't hurt. The war is in its fourteenth year. The cattle are dead and so are the children. There's cholera in the water and pellagra in the bone. And you say you have a problem. She has a problem too. Her ribs are sticking through her skin.

FARMER. You talk too much. Which one's Lvov?

GISELA. You are bad-mannered, but that doesn't matter. *(Suddenly he slaps GISELA in the face. She is silent. She takes out a handkerchief and dabs her mouth. LVOV goes towards him.)*

LVOV. If we embarrass you, perhaps it is because you are ashamed.

FARMER. I want advice.

LVOV. I don't give advice.

ANNA. There is a shed near the soup kitchen. It has a notice on it which says Advice. Or you could ask the gipsies. Or the comrades. They all give advice. *(Pause. The FARMER turns to go.)*

LVOV. What have you done? Killed somebody? *(He stops.)* Unfortunately I am not free tonight. As you can see, I am giving supper here tonight. *(He starts to go.)* You could have done a dozen murders, but I'm not free tonight.

FARMER. I'll wait.

LVOV. You are very patient, but tomorrow I shan't be —

FARMER. I said I'll wait. *(He sits on the floor.)* I've sat by cows all night and got a dead calf for it. So this is nothing. The soldiers made me stand for eighteen hours. So this is nothing. And often, I'm drunk and lie in ditches days on end. So this is nothing.

*Pause. Suddenly* LVOV *flies at the* FARMER, *seizing him and thrusting him out of the room. In a single, continuous movement he returns and leaps onto a chair. The* FARMER *shouts and hammers on the door.*

LVOV. Losing the knack. The knack going. Losing the gift. The gift going. Finding it false and only forty-two. Come nearer those at the back! Those at the back file through! And the voice! The voice going! To hear me you must hardly breathe! Whoever coughs is not engaged, all coughers will be suffocated by their neighbours, you rob them of the right to hear, you rob them, shh! How rare this is, how rare to hear a teacher when the teachers are all dead, the teachers and the poets are all dead, instead we praise the actors, the geniuses posing for the cameras, how effortless they are and charming, this never-ageing charm will be the death of us, only catastrophe can keep us clean **no more geniuses in white suits**, his garden, his summerhouse, his paddock and his rural bench, his **passionate conviviality**, no, where are the teachers, you are so fortunate, you really are, so terribly fortunate, though the knack is going and I am only forty-two, the knack has gone, but I was never young, never, never young and at the brothel wept, I never laughed, I have no wit, the wit died in my jaw, how wonderful the absence of all wit, I sit so still and never tap my feet **never trust the foot tappers** or touch a stranger intimately and at the dance-hall wept, yes, wept, I am so tired of rebels, I the rebel am so tired, are you not tired of being asked to rise, rise up, no stoop, you stoop show me your stooping I will not rise for anyone who cannot stoop say to the hero in the funny hat, you will observe I have no hat, no aspect of what passes for my personality requires a hat and if the sun is hot I seek the shade, it is simplicity you lack and in exchange they give you comedy, I never made a joke, I never ever made a joke, **this terrible deformity of laughter** makes you ugly, no, do not heed the order rise, cease laughing and pay your taxes — *(A* MAN *has entered, scrupulously silent.)* You're late. *(The* MAN *smiles.)* Not late. But certainly you cut it fine.

FORJACKS. I have excuses. But when were you ever interested in excuses? You must make what you want of the fact that I am very nearly late. Though not precisely so. *(He removes his coat. The door is beaten violently.)* You have so many enemies. Some of these enemies are insane. But others are brilliant analysts, it must be said.

LVOV *(climbing off the chair).* And the one outside?
　　What is he?
FORJACKS. He believed in you, and you gave him nothing.
IVORY. **Who says he has to give something! What is he, a scavenger? What is he, a jackal? Stop banging, jackal or I'll bite your liver.** *(The* FARMER *ceases banging.)*
LVOV *(to* FORJACKS*).* All the same, I'm sorry you're late.
ANNA. He's not late!
LVOV. No, he isn't late, but I feel he is —
ANNA. That's ridiculous, he's —
LVOV. **I said I feel he is late.**
FORJACKS. If you wanted me to come earlier, I wish you'd said —
GISELA. That would have ruined the point of it. He wanted you to appear impatient. *(Pause.)*
FORJACKS. Yes *(Pause.)* Yes. *(Pause.)* You once said — I wrote it down —
ANNA. You write everything down!
FORJACKS. Yes — of course I do — be early for your enemies, and late for your friends — *(He looks at* DORA.*)* Did you write that down?
DORA. I don't remember, I —
FORJACKS. I did write that down, and now —
GISELA. It's clearly redundant. Strike it out. In any case, Lvov isn't a friend.
FORJACKS. No . . . No, he isn't, I'll strike it out. *(He grins nervously.)* The traffic is impossible! And the refugees! How easily they die! But always in the most inconvenient positions, a plane had strafed a column of — *(He stops.)* That's odd . . . *(Pause.)* I was about to describe in graphic detail something that I thought appalled me, but actually — *(Pause.)* I wanted to entertain you — *(Pause.)* We do love this war, don't we? We do love suffering . . .

*A train passes. They are still as its many wagons rattle past. During this, a* FIGURE *enters, rotund in a mass of dirty coats. He is still, and waits. The train fades.*

LVOV *(looking at* APOLLO*).* Oh, if there were a single life of love . . . this man who carried girls from bedroom windows and laid them in the clover half asleep, who serviced guns bigger than houses and sent their shells to unknown targets of innocence, and smashed himself, was sawn through the skull by surgeons in a bloody tent, so his naked brain pulsed in the ash-strewn air, and returning, with his clumsy finger round a pencil stub, wrote poems small and shining like impecunious stars . . . if there is a single life of love, it's him . . . *(Pause. He bows.)*
APOLLO. I could have introduced myself better. And you have nicked my style. But.
ANNA. Squeeze me! *(He goes to* ANNA, *embraces her.)* No, squeeze! *(He crushes her.)* You stink! Oh, God, you stink!
DORA. All men adore big men. And all women. Lvov adores Apollo. Anna adores Apollo. And I must admit, I adore him, too. Why?

GISELA. I don't adore him. I feel for Apollo — what, exactly — I feel — gratified that he exists. That's all.

APOLLO. A poem for Gisela.

GISELA. Oh, no —

ANNA. Yes! A poem for Gisela!

APOLLO. Shh!

GISELA. I don't want a —

ANNA ETC. **Shh.** *(Pause.)*

APOLLO. Her ribs will be a source of needles in the new stone age . . . *(Pause.)* That's all. *(He turns to* LVOV.*)* Lvov, how quiet you have been, though I live near, I catch no sounds of you . . .

ARNOLD. He has been ill.

APOLLO. So have we all! And now, this invitation!

LVOV. I have been sitting in the dark.

APOLLO. Excellent, but how quiet you have been . . . *(He turns to them all.)* It is wonderful to see us all again! Conventional sentiment, but it is, it is! Sometimes we must give vent to common sentiments, we must endow the truism with life, Lvov, are you in pain? *(He goes to* LVOV, *holds him.)* Before you, I could not understand why I ached even as I laughed, I could not understand the cruelty which flowed over my lip even in the midst of my condolences, nor the brevity of kindness . . . are you in pain? *(Pause.* SUSANNAH *enters, bearing a table.)* Let me carry a table! Brute to bear the tables! Brute! *(*SLOMAN *follows her in, with a table.)*

SLOMAN. She isn't weak!

APOLLO. I merely demonstrate the absurdity of the convention . . .

SUSANNAH. Table cloths! *(*ARNOLD *goes out, for cloths.)*

FORJACKS. Lvov, every day I thought of you. Every day, I think. I ran through my little book, the diary that I call the Book of Lvov. Sometimes I read things which either I had copied wrongly, or which entirely contradicted other things. And I felt extremely angry, with myself, at first, and then, with you.

SLOMAN. Table cloths! *(He flings them out with a crack. Activity.)*

FORJACKS. For example, the concepts of gratification and abstinence.

SUSANNAH. Thirteen places!

SLOMAN. Thirteen chairs!

GISELA. Privilege expresses itself in different ways in different places. Given the shortage of firewood, to assemble thirteen chairs is reckless extravagance! *(*PEOPLE *carry in chairs of odd kinds.)*

FORJACKS. In June you said — *(He thumbs through a filthy book.)*

ANNA. Chair!

FORJACKS. Shh! *(He thumbs.)* In June you said — yes — Tolerance is impossible without gratification — though you later — not just later, often — questioned the value of tolerance — but then in September — **Please don't deliberately knock into me** — sorry — in September — here it is — the 12th — and I may have got this wrong — you say — the knowledge of lack, when fulfilment is still possible — an orchard which a man chooses not to trespass in — produces a state of imaginative intensity which reality fails to satisfy, at least only in recollection, so that —

what that suggests to me is the essential failure of all moments of consumption, but isn't that opposed to the first proposition, or am I — *(Pause. LVOV doesn't respond.)* Please don't bang me with that chair! *(Pause.)* I suppose I am trying to be consistent which in itself is — *(Pause.)* Yes — that's the point, isn't it — as you said in April, the very attempt to inflict symmetrical systems is an oppression — **Anna!** *(She laughs.)* I will collect a chair, I have every intention of —

APOLLO. The worst chair —

FORJACKS. The worst chair obviously, because I chose to think when grabbing was the order — *(The CHORUS appears to LVOV.)*

IVORY. The chair of nails —

FORJACKS. The worst possible chair, of course — *(APOLLO holds one up.)* That's got no legs!

CHORUS. **Lvov**
**Even the blind see**
**And doubt comes to the infatuated**
**Lvov** *(A cloud of laughter.)*

LVOV. How can I hear myself!

CHORUS. **Lvov**
**We are the people**
**And the people see your slipping self**
**Give us a slogan**
**We love a slogan**
**We will carve your slogan on the bridge**
**Why don't you give us a slogan you snob** *(A cloud of laughter.)*
**Are you afraid?**
**We also are afraid**
**We stand behind our doors with pokers** *(A cloud of laughter.)*
**You knock the weak aside**
**We can't have that!**
**You ridicule the masses**
**We can't have that!** *(Pause. A sound of desolation.)*

LVOV. I am not afraid of death. I am afraid of being revealed. . .


### THE THIRD PARABLE
#### The Economy of the Itinerant Player

*A* POOR FIGURE *enters, blind, and with a violin. He stops, plays a few bars. Pause. He plays a few more bars, stops.*

VIOLINIST. Nobody here, then? *(He moves around the stage, stops, plays, ceases.)*
Nobody here, either?
I have got off the road.
Blind, and off the road.
I heard the guns. That's the way, I said, to the guns. Always to the guns. There is charity. And then they stopped. They stopped and started

somewhere else. That is their way. But now it is days since I heard anything. Only a fool comes off the road. **Is that someone?** *(He immediately begins playing, but stops, an ear cocked.)* No, I am in trouble and no mistake. I broke the cardinal rule. **Oi!** *(He waves the bow.)* **Do you like Strauss?** They laugh at Strauss. But Strauss knew. He knew their emptiness. He knew their hunger for oblivion. **Oi!** *(Pause. A* NUN *appears, looks at him. The* VIOLINIST *plays some bars, and ceases. Pause.)* You do not applaud because you think applause will put you under an obligation. But frankly, I would be content with the applause. *(The* NUN *begins to creep away.)* **Oh, come on, cunt!** *(She stops.)* What are you, a deserter? *(Pause.)* I tell you this. A blind gipsy can hunt down a sighted man and cut his veins swifter than a kite plucks up a rabbit. I also carry a knife. *(Pause.)*

NUN. I can't help you.

VIOLINIST. What are you, a mother? If you're in milk, I'd suck and never mind the money . . .

NUN. I'm a youth, and in a terrible hurry.

VIOLINIST. Don't go, youth. . .

NUN. I must — *(She turns. Suddenly the* VIOLINIST *snaps his bow across his knee. He holds it out in two pitiful sections. The* NUN *stares.)* You have broken your . . . how will you . . . **You are blackmailing me!**

VIOLINIST. An expression of frustration, it occurs to all the great performers.

NUN. Liar, it's a blackmail. It's a blackmail and I won't submit. *(She turns to go. He remains standing, arm outstretched. She stops.)* It is so unjust! I protest!

VIOLINIST. What have you got in your purse?

NUN. Hardly a thing.

VIOLINIST. Half each.

NUN. I am on a mission of mercy and —

VIOLINIST. Me too. The perpetuation of the world. *(He drops the instrument and holds out a dirty hand.)* Anyway, you might have been waylaid, further up the field. This may be merciful.

NUN *(giving him a biscuit)*. You have all the answers.

VIOLINIST *(pocketing the biscuit)*. Let's get on, I will hold your shoulder. *(He holds the* NUN's *shoulder.)* You are frail. What are you, a brother? *(Pause.)* Give me your habit, brother. I am hanging out the holes of this lousy garment. *(Pause.)*

NUN. I can't do that.

VIOLINIST. Why not?

NUN. It is my identity. It is God's. And not mine to give.

VIOLINIST. Do you love Bartok? I would play Bartok, but he brings tears to my eyes. Take it off. He pleads for the unloved. Off with it, now. *(Pause. Then the* NUN *disrobes.)*

NUN. Now let me go — *(Suddenly the* VIOLINIST *bears her to the ground.)* Oh!

VIOLINIST. **I must live! I must live!**

NUN. Oh! *(A voice from offstage.)*

McSTAIN. Hey . . .!

VIOLINIST. Five days and never a soul! Five days and now — surplus!

McNOY *(off)*. Hey! *(The* VIOLINIST *ceases to rape. The* SOLDIERS *enter, look at the sight.)*

MacATTLEE. A nun with no garments . . . *(The* VIOLINIST, *sitting, begins to pluck a tune in pizzicato. The* NUN *sits up.)*

McNOY. Where there is a nun, there must be a convent.

MacATTLEE *(to* VIOLINIST*)*. Have I seen you before?

VIOLINIST. I have heard you before.

MacATTLEE. I have. You play Bartok! You brought tears to my eyes!

VIOLINIST. I can. I can do that. But only with a bow. *(He shows the broken bow.)*

MacATTLEE. Who broke the bow?

VIOLINIST. Ask her. *(They look to the* NUN, *who is dressing.)*

MacATTLEE. You broke the bow? You broke the blind man's bow?

ALL SOLDIERS. We kill nobody —

MacATTLEE. Luckily for you. And I could have done with a little Bartok at this time of day. In the setting sun. When it is obvious the war will not end today after all. These are the hours you need to weep a little.

VIOLINIST. Open your knapsacks. Lend us a bite.

McNOY. There is nothing in our knapsacks. The fact we carry them at all is testimony to our unextinguishable optimism.

VIOLINIST *(standing)*. I'll march with you, then. Soldiers always find the roads. And what's a beggar without roads?

McSTAIN. This is the road.

VIOLINIST. This is the road? They are not what they used to be, then . . . *(They start to move.)*

NUN. Don't go without me!

VIOLINIST. Don't go? But you have a mission.

NUN. No. I never had a mission. I was running away. *(Pause.)*

VIOLINIST. Hold my shoulder, then, and if we meet peasants they will trust you, because of your habit. Then we can rob them better.

ALL SOLDIERS. **Thus we might all survive.**

### END OF THE THIRD PARABLE


*They are arranging the tables. A* GIRL *enters. They stop.*


ELLA. Not missed.
   Not mentioned.
   And not missed.
   **There comes a time the silent want to burst!**

LVOV. Yes . . . it's perfectly true, I had forgotten you. *(She closes her eyes.)* I could have eaten, and slept, and woke, and still would not have said, she isn't here, Ella. It's testimony to our contempt for you.

APOLLO. Oh, no, it —

LVOV. It's clear, for all of us, you have failed to make yourself either loved or hated.

ELLA. Yes.

LVOV. It must be you who is to blame for it.

ELLA. Yes.

APOLLO. No, this is terrible, this is —

LVOV. No, don't apologize! She needs no, and asks for no, nor credits any **apology.**

APOLLO. I am ashamed —

LVOV. No, it is her, let her be ashamed. *(Pause.)*

ELLA. I find it hard to speak. So terribly hard. *(Pause. ANNA goes to embrace her.)*

LVOV. No, no! Let her endure it! *(ELLA shakes her head, agonized.)*

SLOMAN. We had forgotten you, but that doesn't mean you aren't welcome . . . *(JUDITH laughs out loud.)* What's funny? **What's funny!**

JUDITH. You engineer the perfect compromise. You engineer.

SLOMAN. What's wrong with it?

JUDITH. Compromise?

SLOMAN. Yes!

JUDITH. It is a lovely thing in politics, and an ugly thing in art, a miserable thing in marriage and in friendship — I don't know. I have never had a friend. What does Ella think?

ELLA. **I want to burst.**

JUDITH. Yes, we know that.

ELLA. I want words, and sentences to splash all over you. I want my self to come out and say **This is Ella. It is impossible to ignore Ella.**

ANNA. What words? *(ELLA shakes her head.)*

ELLA. I am impossible to love.

SUSANAH. For some, that might make you lovable.

ELLA. No. Lvov is right. Until I exist, I am contemptible. *(She sits on the floor, crossing one leg.)*

SLOMAN. We are being so — utterly and appallingly —

GISELA. Oh, do stop rasping out this useless and repetitive, unfocused and implacable **sympathy!**

ELLA. Yes, please, it's no help to me . . . *(Pause, APOLLO throws her a cushion. They continue laying out the tables. MARYA enters, with a blood-stained dress.)*

MARYA *(lifting it to show)*. The amputees! *(She lets it fall, laughs.)* I carry their limbs to the hut. We pile them in the hut. The hut is bursting and the door has to be forced. I am simply not strong enough. I say to the sentry, come on, help me shut the hut! We put our backs to it. Lvov, this is a funny sight! This fat-backed soldier and this skinny girl, shutting the house of legs!

ARNOLD. There are eleven chairs, and Ella has a cushion.

MARYA. Ella?

ARNOLD. Has a cushion, yes.

MARYA. Who's Ella? Oh, Ella! I want to sit next to Lvov.

LVOV. I am not sitting.

SUSANNAH. Not sitting?

MARYA. All right, then I'll —

SUSANNAH. **Not sitting?**
LVOV. No, nor eating. *(She stares at him.)*
ARNOLD. It's a supper, you said, the final —
SUSANNAH. **Not eating.** *(Pause.)*
LVOV *(deliberately)*. No.
SUSANNAH. I could — *(He smiles.)* Why are you smiling — I could — **You wound and wound** — why do you —
ARNOLD. You shouldn't do it, he only —
SUSANNAH. **I feed him.** *(Pause.)* If you knew what I —
LVOV. Yes, I do know —
FORJACKS. We'll share out what he —
SUSANNAH. **I feed him.** *(Pause.)*
DORA *(to LVOV)*. Please, take a little of what she —
LVOV. No. *(SUSANNAH stares at him. Suddenly, a fast train.)*
APOLLO *(looking at it)*. The officers! *(He salutes. Lights flash on his face. It goes. SUSANNAH has not moved, or taken her eyes from LVOV.)*
APOLLO. They die,
They die,
So perfectly they die,
And I lend them the perfect velvet
Of my incredulity . . . *(Pause.)*
Blue. The colour of my incredulity, I lay beneath immaculately coiffured heads. We shall never see such heads again. My own was opened. Out hopped Pity! *(Pause.)* I drove my car the night the war began, to hear Lvov. Dogs barked along the frontier and lights on mountain sides simmered behind blinds. The wind splashed me like a syphon. Soon we would be dead, or idiots. What a night! What a car! And Lvov, who then was very vain, was wearing blue, which clung to his body like a veil on the wet face of a widow, the beautiful Lvov, struggling to discard, but never able to. . .
FORJACKS. He never denied the power of materiality, did you Lvov? He was never less than human. Did he not say austerity was a flagellation, a mark of hatred of the world and of the body?
IVORY. I flagellate.
FORJACKS. You do —
IVORY. I flagellate, yes.
FORJACKS. Yes, yes, you do . . . *(They are seated, but for LVOV, SUSANNAH, SLOMAN. SUSANNAH goes out.)*
DORA. Gisela, your hands are like cut flowers. You lay down your hands as if they were not joined to you. You place them. You arrange them like cut flowers.
APOLLO. How beautiful it is, this table cloth. No wonder you lay your hands like flowers. What does it matter if the menu stinks, we have a table cloth white as a glacier, stiff as a glacier . . . I used to sit in cafés with one glass . . . an oasis in a white landscape . . . all's well if the launderers are busy . . .!

ANNA. I brought the cloth. We fuck in table cloths. *(JUDITH laughs.)* We do! Obviously, there are no sheets, and since even the basest lout craves the false intimacy of sheets, we fuck in these . . .

IVORY. The lout wants his buttocks covered.

ANNA. He wants them covered, yes, and we found a hotel bombed. So much damask! So much stiff and monogrammed! But short. Our feet protrude . . .!

FORJACKS. It has all the logic of imperfect sex . . .

IVORY. **What's imperfect about it! What!**

FORJACKS. The comic dimensions of imperfect sex . . .

IVORY. **What's comic about it? You know no sex, comic or otherwise!**

ARNOLD. All right, all right . . .

IVORY. He sits there —

ARNOLD. All right, all right . . .

IVORY. He sits there, he sits there . . .

MARYA. Shh . . . Shh . . . *(A profound pause. They look, their looks are drawn toward LVOV.)*

LVOV. You came. All of you came. Even through contempt and dwindling fascination. I assembled you for a final act of love, but seeing you, it's obvious you haven't any more sufficient love for what's required —

*The* CHORUS *asserts itself.*

CHORUS. **Are you trying**
**You are trying to escape**
**Lvov**
**Lvov**
**You aren't trying**

LVOV. They look at me like —

CHORUS. **Wrong words**
**Try other words then**

LVOV. You can see they think I'm —

CHORUS. **Any old excuse will do**

LVOV. They are feeling sorry for me —

CHORUS. **How right it is that you should die then**

LVOV. I know that, I have established that —

CHORUS. **New words, then!** *(Pause.* LVOV *sits on the floor.)* The Museum of the Masses will consist of ninety rooms, beginning with the wheel and ending with space travel. Our rise. Our painful ascent. The photographs show crowds attending rallies and funerals and carnivals at which. Our rise. Our painful ascent. In these photographs the faces of individuals are obscured by magnification. Our rise. Our. *(The cloud of laughter.)*

LVOV. **I am turning their love into hate.** *(Pause.)* It's difficult. I am so lovable. You can see, how difficult it is . . . *(The door opens. An* OFFICER *enters.)*

OFFICER. This is an illegal gathering. Are you Lvov?

LVOV *(springing into life).* No, Lvov has gone.

OFFICER. Gone where?

LVOV. He left in a car.

OFFICER *(incredulous).* A car? What car?

LVOV. A blue car, with one broken headlight.

OFFICER. You're lying.

LVOV. No! A red car with a roof rack.

OFFICER. A lie remains a lie, no matter how elaborate . . .

LVOV. You have been studying Lvov! His very tone!

OFFICER. I have read Lvov.

LVOV. Not easy, in this climate.

OFFICER. I found a copy in a waiting room.

LVOV. Oh, which? I should love to see it.

OFFICER. The up-line at Varna.

LVOV. Let's go, at once!

OFFICER. I know who you are. Do you think I am an idiot?

LVOV. Obviously it would assist me if you were.

OFFICER. Everything you say proves you are Lvov, and I am proceeding to dismiss this unlawful assembly under the regulations of December 19 —

LVOV. This comic formality becomes you very well —

OFFICER *(turning ferociously).* **I can also be a cunt.** *(Pause.* SLOMAN *enters with a tray and the baked dog.)*

LVOV. Yes, and now I wonder, would you carve the meat for us? *(Pause.)*

OFFICER. Meat? *(*LVOV *nods towards the table. The* OFFICER *drifts towards it.)*

JUDITH *(to* LVOV.*)* How I love you. For a short time I believed I'd seen the last of you. . .

LVOV *(wearily).* The last of me? In which form?

JUDITH. The form I loved.

OFFICER. It's a dog . . .

LVOV. Yes, it's a dog! A bitch mongrel, I understand, but the butcher would know better. There he is holding the carver, Barry, give him the knife . . . *(*SLOMAN *holds out the carving knife. The* OFFICER *looks from face to face. Pause.)*

OFFICER. **I can also be a cunt!** *(They clap. He smiles. Removes his cap and takes the knife.)*

ARNOLD. Everyone wishes to force everyone else to hear him. Even a madman banging a tin with a fork . . .

DORA. Everyone thinks his message is as good as anyone else's . . . Even an idiot calling his number . . .

OFFICER. No meat on this fucking animal. . .

LVOV. Yet no one wishes to be responsible for the condition of the world. That is very understandable. Who would accept the charge?

OFFICER *(impatiently).* Fuck this . . !

LVOV. All the dictators are dead. They could not stand the accusation. The accumulation of evidence shamed even their relentless egos, the deserts of their enterprises, the corpses of their epigones, their cardres stinking in the sun, all their little **red and green books!**

OFFICER *(throwing down the carver).* **Fuck this, I said.**

LVOV. No meat?

OFFICER. No meat. *(He looks at LVOV. He nods towards the door.)*
ANNA *(to OFFICER).* Come outside, I'll show you something.
OFFICER. What you could show me, I have seen before.
ANNA. All right, I'll fall in love with you as well.
OFFICER. You wouldn't be the first. *(She smiles.)* I like your body, and I like
    your face. but even love could not undo my orders. *(He turns to LVOV.)*
    Lvov — *(He goes to arrest LVOV, but ARNOLD swiftly takes him by the
    throat. Everyone watches as he slowly bears the OFFICER to the floor,
    throttling him. The OFFICER's knees fold under him. He is let to the
    floor. ARNOLD walks to a chair and sits, his hands hanging at his sides.)*
LVOV. He was wrong. Love can. *(They don't move, but look at ARNOLD.
    ARNOLD weeps, his shoulders heaving.)* Arnold, since you were already
    a murderer, how can I praise you? — You did no more than Anna might
    have done in fornicating by the shed.
ARNOLD. For a fiction . . . ! For a fiction . . . !
IVORY. We are all murderers here.
LVOV. Exactly. So a killing is no sacrifice.
ARNOLD *(standing).* **It was a sacrifice! It was a sacrifice.**
GISELA. My wrists are like reeds. *(She looks at them.)* Reeds!
ARNOLD. **Why do I require you? Why do I need you? I hate you.**
GISELA. You couldn't hurt a fly with these . . .
ARNOLD. I could so easily — I could —
LVOV. Yes.
ARNOLD. **So easily.**


### THE FOURTH PARABLE
#### The Consolations of Accumulations

*A* WOMAN *enters dragging a strung bundle. She sits on it. The cloud of
laughter passes. The sound of music on an ancient gramaphone. A* MAN
*dances to a waltz with an imaginary partner. He stops. The* WOMAN *blows
her nose.*

WOMAN. Do you think that's funny?
MAN. My partner is dead. Of an illness I could not diagnose.
WOMAN. What are you, a doctor?
MAN. Yes, but I keep it to myself.
WOMAN. Look at my ulcers, and I won't tell anyone. *(She pulls up her
    skirt.)*
MAN. What beautiful legs.
WOMAN. One day your sarcasm will turn round and slap you in the teeth.
MAN. No, your legs are beautiful. Inelegant, but beautiful. However, I've
    no medicine. *(He pulls down her skirt.)* The task before us is not to cure
    deformity but to describe it differently. That is the function of learning
    in an age of disease.

WOMAN. Excellent. What are you after? A new dancing partner? You're no help to me. *(She gets up.)*

MAN. What's in the parcel?

WOMAN. Loot. I go around the monasteries.

MAN. How funny! You have given yourself ulcers dragging loot through thorns and hedges. You will become infected and die of loot.

WOMAN. Let's dance, for old time's sake . . . *(He winds up the gramaphone.)*

MAN. Because I'm undernourished I do a rather slower step, but the gramaphone is old and matches my retarded style . . .

WOMAN. If I am ridiculous dragging loot through a devastated country, you are equally ridiculous dancing when you are dying. *(They do a few turns. The* THREE SOLDIERS *appear, attracted by the sound. They watch. Suddenly the* MAN *sinks to the floor. The music ceases.)* I asked him to cure my ulcers and all he did was get philosophical. *(She sits.)*

McSTAIN. Is that loot you're sitting on?

WOMAN. Yes, and what if it is? It is, and so what? Of course it's loot, you boggling fool. I am waiting for the restoration of order and the stability of currency. Then I shall sell the loot and enjoy a comfortable retirement.

McNOY. You might as well lug bricks in a bucket.

WOMAN. How do you know it isn't bricks? Bricks are scarce. It might be bricks.

McNOY. The whole lot wouldn't buy a sandwich.

WOMAN. At this moment, obviously. Now, obviously. I admit the likelihood I shall die infected of ulcers. But at least I keep one jump ahead. At least. At least. At least I look to the future. At least I am an optimist. At least.

MACATTLEE. We passed a skull with its gob full of silver.

WOMAN. An optimist. At least he had his faith. *(They turn to go.)* Carry my loot!

MACATTLEE *(stopping, cruelly)*. With hopelessness comes the decline of temper. So whereas at one time I might have struck you for impertinence, now I merely smile, a smile of insipid tolerance . . .

WOMAN. Pick it up then, there's a love.

McNOY. We'll carry you, for your ulcers, but not the loot.

WOMAN. The loot also.

McSTAIN. No loot.

WOMAN. What am I without the loot?

McSTAIN. How would I know?

WOMAN. Nothing. Nothing without the loot, I promise you. *(They drift away.)* Oh pity me! Pity an optimist! *(They stop. The wind blows. Pause.)*

McSTAIN. We were ever open to persuasion.

MACATTLEE. We were ever open.

McNOY. We have found education in the strangest places.

WOMAN. You! With the broad back! Parcel! You! With the long arms! Stoop! *(They obey.)*

### *END OF THE FOURTH PARABLE*

LVOV. Take the food outside and leave it on the pavement. *(Pause.)*

SLOMAN. What is he —

LVOV. Take the food outside and leave it on the —

SLOMAN. **What!** *(Pause.)*

GISELA. You heard what he said —

SLOMAN. **I heard** —

LVOV. The pavement, yes. You will have food, but take that food and leave it on the pavement.

FORJACKS. Wouldn't it be better to —

LVOV. Don't look for the poor. Let whoever finds it, eat it. If it is an extortionist, so be it. Or a plump actor, give it to him. It humiliates to choose between the starving, just as to cure one man's blindness while another passes on the other side is to play the arbitrary among arbitrariness. **Who loves me, then? What is the proof of love but doing the undoable?** *(They watch him, holding their plates and reluctant.)* You don't believe I shall provide? You want it proved. I don't prove anything. Never. **When did we ever prove?** No, proof's for the mob. We abhorred the command to prove, which is the wall to freedom . . . *(They hang back, staring at the plates. He looks to* SUSANNAH.*)* How she hates me . . ! *(He laughs.)* And him! *(He looks at* SLOMAN. *Some drift out of the door.)*

IVORY *(to* LVOV). All my life, I think I wanted to be other people. And seeing you, I wanted to be you. I still do. I move like you. Look, this gesture — my arm like this — is pure imitation. That can't be freedom, can it? Freedom must be ceasing to be you. *(He goes out.)*

DORA. Have you noticed, how we deteriorate? I saw it, the moment we came in, the deterioration. We all of us were — silently, but — actually — shocked! We didn't say, but looked, peering in the oily light for what we had been once. Only you were still the same. You — shone! You know, don't you, the shame that fastens to the liver of life in the presence of the abstentionist? And you licensed everything, only forbidding yourself, **it isn't right, is it**? Coming together and seeing ourselves, well, you've got to be honest, we have all — *(She shudders.* GISELA *comes to her.)* No, I'm all right, I'm perfectly all right, I am merely being honest, which is arguably a sign I'm not all right at all . . . *(She goes out with her plate, swiftly. Others return, empty-handed, then* DORA *returns, boldly.)* The beauty of Lvov was that he arrived complete. He sprang from — where — I don't know — who knows where he sprang from — and was **complete**. The question is however, whether we admire completeness. Whether we might not rather admire — flexibility, growth, deterioration, alteration, because man must, you see, he must —

APOLLO. Suffer.

DORA *(Pause. She shrugs).* I don't know. Suffer? Yes.

LVOV. You are betraying me. *(He sits at the table, alone. They are standing. Pause. They look at one another.)* Not one of you. All of you. *(Pause.)* But one. *(Pause.)*

ANNA. We are very hungry, and to put the food —

LVOV. **Never mind the food.** *(Pause.)* Tell me how you will betray me. Anna. *(Pause.)*

ANNA. Me?

LVOV. Yes. How?

ANNA. Me — I —

LVOV. Think how.

ANNA. I —

SLOMAN. Yes, think! *(Pause.)*

ANNA. By marrying a glamorous idiot who will ruin my life. *(Pause.)* He will make me his thing. We will dance in the lights and imitate love. I will trivialize myself. That's betrayal, isn't it?

MARYA. I shall become kind. *(Pause. They look at her.)* **Well, that's betrayal!** *(Pause.)*

SLOMAN. I, obviously, by going down into the street and preaching the likeness of all men. The commonness of all things. In my heart, I have already begun the elimination of Lvov. I have put his power under the light and seen it to be the desperate clamour of a lonely child . . . *(Pause.)*

LVOV. How difficult it is for you . . . *(Pause.)* Gisela . . . how will you?

GISELA. By being happy, I suppose . . .

ANNA. Yes! Yes! That's what he hates! Isn't it, Lvov?

JUDITH. What happiness?

ANNA. That's what gives Lvov the horrors —

JUDITH. **What happiness.** *(Pause.)*

GISELA. The aching for the absent thing might die . . . and in its place there might be . . . a continuing fascination with the existent . . .

JUDITH. Theory.

GISELA. Theory, yes. Since I am all absence. Since I am made of absence. A theory, obviously. *(Pause.)*

LVOV. Ivory? *(Pause.)*

IVORY. By killing mundanely. By being ashamed. By repeating slogans invented by Sloman —

SLOMAN. Oh, all right —

IVORY. **By being skinned and cooked by Sloman —**

SLOMAN. All right, all right —

IVORY. Shh, I am as ambitious as you, shh, I am, I am . . . *(Pause. Then APOLLO occupies the silence.)*

APOLLO. It's true, that at moments of tiredness I long to sit under a tree with a dog. The dog's feet in my lap and its eyes on the moon. I long to hear the train on the incline, reaching for the villages. . . *(Suddenly he kneels to LVOV.)* Master! Master! The pleasure it gives to call him **Master!** *(He hangs his head penitently.)* I come to you because you will not ridicule the hunger that I feel for the woman on the corner of the avenue whose skirt lies flat over her belly like a flag on a corpse. **Master!** I lost the top of my head but I came back, who else would justify the pain? **Master!** *(He gets up.)* And Lvov is inferior to me. Both in language and imagination. I know all Lvov by heart.

FORJACKS. It is impossible to know Lvov by heart.

APOLLO. I do. It's my betrayal.

FORJACKS. It's not possible.

APOLLO. All the same, I do.

FORJACKS. Rubbish, with all respect. . .
APOLLO. **With no respect I know it.** Beg me, I will quote.
FORJACKS. It's beyond the —
APOLLO. **Beg me.** *(Pause.)*
FORJACKS. On Pity, then.
APOLLO. Which?
FORJACKS. On Pity given at —
APOLLO. You don't know yourself! The titles, even!
FORJACKS. Wait!
APOLLO. He barely knows the titles!
FORJACKS. At Rotterdam.
APOLLO. Noon or Night?
IVORY. Night!
APOLLO. It begins with an aphorism. The aphorism is, 'Pity is Theft'. It
    continues on the theme of the right to suffering, as follows, 'She who
    hides her pain conspires in the infliction of the wound that follows — '
FORJACKS. That's not all of it —
APOLLO. Of course it's not all of it, do you want all of it? I will give you all
    of it.
LVOV. No one admires you. They think you sycophantic and absurd.
APOLLO. I am absurd, and therefore cannot be insulted.
LVOV. You have learned the art of the parrot.
APOLLO. I am a parrrot and therefore cannot be insulted.
LVOV. And if I repudiate my words?
APOLLO. They stay.
FORJACKS *(heated)*. On Violence!
APOLLO. On Violence, given at the Village on the River San.

*The* CHORUS *appears to* LVOV.

LVOV. How absurd! How contemptible they are!
CHORUS. **Soon be free.**
LVOV. How could you hope to satisfy them?
CHORUS. **Soon be free.**
LVOV. They hate me, all of them. But they haven't the courage to act on their
    hatred —
CHORUS. **Soon.**
LVOV. I wound them and they still —
CHORUS. **Soon.**
LVOV. All right!
CHORUS. **Easy to die when you don't love.**
LVOV. That's what you say . . . *(The cloud of laughter.)* They must kill me.
    I cannot kill myself.
CHORUS. **They'll kill you.**
LVOV. They will? But they love me, no matter how I hurt them, they still —
CHORUS. **Hurt them more —**
LVOV. They won't, they —
CHORUS. **They long to, yes!**

LVOV. I am not afraid of death only oblivion! *(Laughter again.)* Do you think I lived this terrible life to be forgotten?

CHORUS. **We march across the landscape singing**

LVOV. Shut up —

CHORUS. **We tar the women in short skirts and blind the men in glasses**

LVOV. I defy your power of forgetting!

CHORUS. **Child of the people**
  **Lvov**
  **Son of the people**

*Pause. Sound of the landscape.*

ELLA *(from under the table, where she has hidden herself).* I killed my child. Is anybody listening? I did it in a railway carriage. It had no ticket. It should have had a ticket, shouldn't it? I think the way this war has made people cunning is the most sickening thing and never paying your debts and scrounging and skyving is the rule not the exception, the pleasure in settling one of them I could not begin to tell you **no ticket well that's your. Scrounging, well this time you**. I had one, of course. I, who have not two halfpennies to rub together, I got one at some sacrifice and if more people did the same then. *(Pause.)*

  It was obvious, Lvov, you would attract to you all those for whom the normal state of life was nauseating, the mad, the critical, the lawless, the impatient, and that this very following by its character, would discredit you with those who form the mass of our society. Can you explain how you intend to move from the minority to the majority? *(The cloud of laughter.)* You have been years and still we're twelve. Forjacks was a torturer and there are several murderers among us, it is an unappetising clique and rather dirty. The women are whores and if they're not they wish to be —

DORA. I have no wish to be —

ELLA. You would with him —

DORA. I deny —

ELLA. **You would with him** —

DORA. Oh —

ELLA. Kiss me! Kiss me, do! *(She throws her arms round* DORA. *Pause.)* Life was, and ever shall be, of no significance! And yet, desperately, we will discriminate! For example, in the doling out of charity, I fill the spoon more fully for the beautiful orphan. This seems to me not only inevitable, but correct. *(Pause. She sits neatly on the floor.)*

SUSANNAH. Are we going to eat?

IVORY. He said —

SUSANNAH. **I said are we going to eat.**

## THE FIFTH PARABLE
### How the Child Was Lost

*The* THREE SOLDIERS *enter.*

ALL. We thought we had a child. We thought we were pregnant.

MCSTAIN. How this thought came about.

MACATTLEE. For six weeks we saw nothing but the dead.

MCNOY. Perhaps because we walked in circles.

MACATTLEE. This was a suspicion. But coming again upon the dead, such was the speed of their deterioration you could not say —

MCSTAIN. With any certainty —

MACATTLEE. With any certainty, this cadavre I have seen before.

MCNOY. What with the seasons changing, wild grasses and heathers struggling through the limbs forced them in new positions so —

MCSTAIN. This remains hypothetical —

MCNOY. Nevertheless, the thought occurred —

ALL. **We three alone survived.** *(Pause.)*

MCNOY. A sort of ecstasy.

MCSTAIN. Terror at our great inheritance but also —

MACATTLEE. Ecstasy!

ALL. **We rolled upon the bosom of the earth!** *(Pause.)*

MCSTAIN. Until there came upon us a cry of mortality.

MCNOY. In me especially.

MACATTLEE. In him the cry called loudest.

MCNOY. I ached for love beyond the mundane obligations of the squad.

MACATTLEE. He particularly ached.

MCSTAIN. And subsequently suffered.

MCNOY. A stirring in my lower parts I could not identify.

MCSTAIN. The old male anger . . .

MCNOY. No, not that!

MACATTLEE. The hammer of old John . . .

MCNOY. I said not that! *(Pause.)* Then at a cruel hour of the night, a cold, dead hour, it began, and neither of these could be roused, I at my extremity and they in deathly kip, mouths all slobbering the black-toothed bastards . . . I ripped! I ripped! *(A* CHILD *enters.)* Oh, gently, gently, little one! *(He puts his hands on the* CHILD, *and caresses her. An extensive silence. The others wake.)*

MACATTLEE. We woke, and disbelieved!

MCNOY. Look, the comfort of our solitude . . . !

MCSTAIN. What rip?

MCNOY *(showing his flesh).* There.

MCSTAIN. Rip? Where?

MCNOY. **I said there.**

MACATTLEE. Let's not quarrel, we are so few. But your gut is as smooth as the marble on a tomb —

MCNOY. **Re—joice! Re—joice!**

MACATTLEE. Just establishing the fact —

McNOY. Re—joice!

MacATTLEE. The fact — purely for the record —

McNOY *(furiously)*. **Re—joice!**

MacATTLEE. Must — hang on — to — the —

McSTAIN. No criticism —

MacATTLEE. No criticism, but —

McNOY. **Re—joice you bas—tards —**

MacATTLEE. There is no mark on your tummy and I will not pretend there is, all right?

McSTAIN. Oi. *(He looks at the* CHILD. *Their eyes travel.* McNOY's *chanting dies. The* CHILD *has wandered and picked up a bomb. She examines it, tosses it in the air and catches it again.)*

McNOY *(horrified)*. I ripped . . .

MacATTLEE. You did . . . you did rip . . . yes . . . *(She throws it up again.)*

McNOY. **I ripped . . . !**

MacATTLEE/McSTAIN. **All right!** *(The* CHILD *throws it up again.)*

McSTAIN *(crawling towards the* CHILD). What's little baby got there, then? What's baby's lovely thingammy?

McNOY *(lying on his back)*. I dream of fields and swings, I dream of cots and snow white coverlets . . .

MacATTLEE. Mac's ill . . .

McSTAIN. What's baby do-da doing den?

McNOY *(delirious)*. I dream of apple blossom falling on the sunshade . . .

MacATTLEE. Mac's got childbed fever . . . *(The* CHILD *throws up the bomb again.* McSTAIN *falls to the ground, covering his head. The* CHILD *catches the bomb, is entertained.)*

McSTAIN. Show whatsit to old thingammy — *(The* CHILD *tosses it up again.* McSTAIN *cringes to the ground.)*

McNOY. It's tiny fingers grope towards my lips, my breasts ache with milk yet unexpressed, wake! Wake!

MacATTLEE. Oh, Mac, our comrade of so many fallen bells . . .

McSTAIN *(undeterred)*. Teeny weeny turn for palsy, teeny — *(He sees a* WOMAN *from the corner of his eye.)*

WOMAN *(to* CHILD). Oi. Scraparse. Told you not to play with soldiers. In. *(She jerks her thumb. The* CHILD *gets up, goes off, past her.)*

McNOY *(sitting up)*. We thought we were alone in the world . . .

WOMAN. You are. *(She goes off. The* SOLDIERS *pick up their bags.* McNOY *hangs his head, foolishly.* McSTAIN *goes to him, puts an arm round him. They go to leave, when an explosion is heard. They stop. They continue.)*

## END OF THE FIFTH PARABLE

LVOV *(to* GISELA). The way your eyes hang on me. As if I were the first made man.

GISELA. Oh?

LVOV. Hunger or no hunger. You wash me with desire.

GISELA. I don't notice it any more.

LVOV. Yes. I lather in your fascination. It soddens my clothes.

GISELA *(she shrugs, sarcastically)*. You don't miss a thing. *(She goes to a chair, and sits, looking at him.)*

LVOV. Sticky and uncomfortable.

GISELA. Too bad. *(He stares at her. She returns his stare.)*

JUDITH *(breaking the silence)*. You are not as charming tonight as you can be. Is he? Hardly charming at all.

LVOV. You see everything.

JUDITH. It's obvious.

LVOV. And feel nothing.

JUDITH. Yes. I admit that.

LVOV *(still looking at* GISELA*)*. Nothing but ambition. Which is not a feeling.

JUDITH. You should know.

LVOV. Not a feeling but a lack.

JUDITH. You should know.

LVOV. Gisela.

JUDITH. Charm of a different order, perhaps.

LVOV. Ask Dora. *(Pause.)*

GISELA. What? *(Pause.)*

DORA. Yes, I think you should.

LVOV. Dora knows! Without the least articulation, Dora knows! I have not spent so many bitter hours with this woman for her to fail me now.

DORA. Go with him, if it is what he wants.

LVOV. We sat, and the bitterness ran out of our mouths. We might have bitten the iron rims off tables, Dora and I. *(DORA snatches a laugh.)*

GISELA. Don't play with me. *(JUDITH laughs, peeling.)* **Shut up. Shut up.**

JUDITH *(shaking her head)*. The sentiment . . . I'm sorry . . . the sentiment . . . of course he will play with you . . .

LVOV *(inspired)*. I thought of life as a basket! And in the basket, fruits! Name the fruits!

IVORY. Love.

LVOV. Love.

ANNA. Laughter.

LVOV. Laughter — of a sort —

FORJACKS. Years!

LVOV. Years! Years!

MARYA. Ecstasy.

LVOV. Ecstasy.

DORA. Melancholy.

LVOV. Melancholy, or there could be no ecstasy.

JUDITH. Pain.

LVOV. Pain. But —

APOLLO. Death. *(Pause.)* How you love death. And you have never seen it.

LVOV. Is death bad, then? How bad?

APOLLO. Lvov has never stood under fire. Lvov has never seen the meat. Lvov has never smelled the blood. Lvov has sat in a wooden chair. I say this

without the whisper of a criticism. Lvov has never felt the surgeon's. Lvov
has never seen the widow's. Lvov has slept in a wooden bunk. I say this
without the whisper of. Lvov has never worn bowel as garland. Lvov has
never scraped brain. Or watched boys jerk on strings. And yet I listen to
him with respect. Because it is hard to go where Lvov goes. Cold there, I
think. *(Pause.)*

LVOV *(to* GISELA*).* If you will see me naked, I'll see you . . . *(Pause. She
gets up. They all stare at her. She glares at them boldly.)*

FORJACKS *(with gathering clarity).* I know what you do! I know what you
do! You make all things equal, all categories! You make evil good by
removing the description! But its essence remains the same. Is anybody
listening? That's his method! It's all very well saying his thought is not
exactly thought at all but — something else — that's all very well, maybe
it's not thought but it still requires two things — consistency and — **I am
free of Lvov, I am free, I am free of Lvov!**

ANNA. Be quiet or I'll stab you. *(He stops.* GISELA *goes out with* LVOV*.)*
**Be quiet.** *(Pause.* JUDITH *looks at* ANNA*.)* Lvov — has no communion
with women . . . *(She looks round.)* What's the use if he —
**He denies himself it is a principle!**
And she —
**It's a principle he never —**
What's —
He has no —

JUDITH. Cock?

ANNA. It's there but —
It exists but —
The power is not used it only — *(To* IVORY*.)*
Don't laugh at me, I'll —

IVORY. Was I laughing? I was discerning the contrast between the shadow
and the substance —

ANNA. That's laughter, you male slag —
**How can he be trusted?**

SUSANNAH *(who has watched this icily).* Lvov is killing Lvov . . .

ANNA. **Gisela!**
What's she —
She hangs her education out like some — **great tit** — and as for her — did
you read that — her **formidable mind** — I read it in the paper — the
formidable mind of Gisela Rust — what's she — *(Pause. She sits on the
floor.)* I ask a lot of Lvov. I ask him to be unlike. Utterly **unlike**. And he
said, you must ask more of me, always more. *(Pause.)*
**He makes me feel a prostitute.**
*(Pause. She jumps up.)*
Where are they? *(JUDITH looks at her. Coolly.)* Gisela wears learning
like a strip of chiffon over her arse, who's fooled? Anybody fooled? *(To
DORA.)* You're her — what are you to her?

DORA. I protect her.

ANNA. Do you?
She is a valve.

A valve with learning smeared. With learning dolloped. *(Pause.)*
Protect her, then. *(Pause.)*
My sexuality is thank you perfectly.
I have no sexuality.
Lvov also has none. *(ARNOLD goes to her. She looks at him, touches his face.)*
Arnold, I'm not hungry any more . . . *(She sits at his feet. GISELA enters. She returns to her chair, sits. Pause.)*
GISELA. 'There is no such thing as sin. Merely violence to the self.' Lvov. *(A train comes. MARYA rushes to the window.)*
MARYA. They're coming back — alive! *(Train wheels.)*

### THE SIXTH PARABLE
#### The Fleeting Appearance of an Idealist

*A* SOLDIER *appears holding wild flowers.*

THE GUNNER. Going home.
We picked a certain flower which grew in abundance. A flower as common as men. We pushed the flower down our guns, and walked West. Going home.
LVOV *(entering).* He was not tired of killing. He was tired of killing meaninglessly.
THE GUNNER. I have a child, and an old mother in a room . . .
LVOV. He is not tired of killing. He requires a better excuse.

*The* CHORUS *appears.*

CHORUS. **Still alive?**
  **Still alive, Lvov?**
LVOV. Yes, and out of my time.
CHORUS. **New world, Lvov.**
LVOV. I notice.
CHORUS. **And we shall be**
  **All in one line**
  **Arms linked**
  **The shrill voice of**
  **The popular and**

*The cloud of laughter.*

LVOV. Who could they follow but the one who is not human? Could you worship a human? Follow me, says the messiah. And they chuck away their tools. This way, says the messiah. And they abandon their children. They lock up their rooms and leave their gardens to the weeds. Could you do that for a **human**?

CHORUS. **Still here, Lvov?**

LVOV. It's time, it's time, and now they hate me more than ever they loved . . .

THE GUNNER *(about to throw away his gun)*. Away, gun!

LVOV. No, bury it in oiled rags . . . *(The* GUNNER *thinks. The* THREE SOLDIERS *enter. They see* LVOV *and kneel.)* You only kneel because you do not know me well enough . . .

ALL. We kneel because we are so tired of being upright.

LVOV *(with a laugh)*. Excellent! Listen I was not born with this face, no, I made it. Underneath it lie such long forgotten qualities as charm and mischief, humour, lechery, like tumuli in ancient landscapes, who would stoop to excavate them now? **I made myself terrible.** I am Lvov, do you dare to murder me?

ALL. We kill no — body!

LVOV. Why not? I never forbade it! **It is real power when you are not afraid to die.**

THE GUNNER. We put flowers down our guns and commandeered the train. Home James, we said! The harvest is due and I have a child to kiss. Home James!

LVOV. You were not tired of killing. You required a better excuse. *(A* WOMAN *enters, holding a* CHILD.*)*

WOMAN. I told him, take your tunic off and let me hold your naked body, my thin love, my emaciated love who held back hundreds, tell me in this bed to the sounds of our babies sleeping how you held back hundreds with your gun my thin love, my body aches to hear, my vastness opens to hear how you held back hundreds, poets, criminals, tutors, lathe-turners who fell under your gun you grey-faced thin one, tell me of your concrete and your wire, oh, my own rear-guard . . .

GISELA. How extraordinary to achieve clarity from sheer unhappiness.

But it happens.

How amazing.

You have made me hate my own flesh.

That is — really, that is — criminal — isn't it?

That is surely the very limit of horror?

I terribly hate you and naturally, being an intellectual I have to know the causes — no, don't piss over my need to articulate — **you common bastard** — there — you have elicited from me the most appalling abuse — and all this because I saw you naked and —

**You common bastard** —

You saw me —

How I adored you saying no, your eyes saying, and your closed nature, always no, and how quickly I hated you when you said yes, how rapidly you appeared in your authentic **commonness**.

LVOV. Yes.

GISELA. What did any of us share? You, was it? Just you? I hate you because you held us in contempt.

THE MACS. Can we get up now?

GISELA. And your coldness was only contempt.

THE MACS. Can we get up?

GISELA. **And your sex was only contempt.**

THE MACS. We will, I think . . .

WOMAN. We formed a party to protect the land. And a party to protect the peace. But —

THE GUNNER. Where did you hang my tunic? And my gun, with the withered flower down its spout? Where did you put my gun?

WOMAN. Speaking as a party woman I said, much as I enjoyed your body, now the time has come —

THE GUNNER. Make the flower into a badge. Simplify it. Make a badge.

THE MACS. So we stood up. *(They stand, nervously.* LVOV *laughs.)*

GISELA. I have a choice. If I don't hate you, I have only myself to hate. And I am not going to gnaw myself to naked nerve and bone. (JUDITH *enters.*)

JUDITH. Trust me. (LVOV *looks at her.)* You want to do this all on your own, but I know it's beyond you, Lvov. The dying. Beyond you. *(She sits.)* They've fallen asleep. Not one of them was your equal. And they've fallen asleep.

LVOV. You are my equal, then . . .

JUDITH. Yes. Only me.

LVOV. How did you know? How did you know I intended to die?

JUDITH. You must. It is impossible for you to continue. And if all you have done is not to be turned into dust, and error, yes, you must. They have got the measure of you, Lvov.

LVOV. I know.

JUDITH. They parody you. The clever ones.

LVOV. I thought as much.

JUDITH. Yes. They do you very well. And the ones who are not clever complain at your ingratitude.

LVOV. They are only human.

JUDITH. They are human, and you are tired.

LVOV. Am I? Am I tired? Yes, I am tired. Terribly tired. **I am so lonely, hold my hands.** *(She kneels by him, holding his hands.)* What do you want?

JUDITH. To know.

LVOV. Yes . . .

JUDITH. I alone of all of them, I truly want to know. I alone, prefer knowledge to peace. You taught me everything. Everything. But one thing you cannot teach me is what it is to live without you. And that I have to know. I want to help you to die, so that there is no one left. And after you there won't be. Anyone at all. Only cacophony. And then I shall be solely responsible. The sole proprietor of my mind. So you see, I have to know. That is real, and pure, and utter curiosity. It was inevitable, wasn't it, that one of us would take your words to heart?

LVOV. **Don't fall asleep!**

JUDITH. I won't . . . I won't fall asleep . . . *(She holds him.)*

THE MACS *(to the* GUNNER*).* Off we go then . . . *(Pause.)* Do we . . .?

THE GUNNER. I came home, to a new world . . .

THE MACS. We always do.

THE GUNNER. No, this was newer, though it contained the old . . .

THE MACS. It always does.

THE GUNNER. And this world. **This** world, belonged to me.

THE MACS. This one. Definitely, this one.

THE GUNNER. For this one I will die. And if necessary, make others die.

THE MACS. Which way?

THE GUNNER. For this, I take up the loathed gun.

THE MACS. **The loathed gun.**

WOMAN. No longer loathed.

THE GUNNER. Defender of my child. I oil its parts with such reverence . . .

WOMAN. Come back victorious, or not at all. *(He kisses her. Shoulders his gun, sets out.)*

THE MACS. Erm . . .*(He stops.)* Erm . . .*(He looks.)* The bell order, is it still in force?

THE GUNNER. Bell order?

MacATTLEE. The compulsory unslinging of all bells. *(He looks confused.)*

THE MACS *(crossly)*. **The bell order.**

WOMAN. And seeing him, his loved hands, for fear of calling him and cradling him and hiding him inside myself **I resolutely turn my back** . . .

LVOV. I was shallow. I was juvenile. I said things others had said before me.

JUDITH. I remember.

LVOV. It was only slowly I came to perfection.

JUDITH. Briefly. Wonderfully.

LVOV. And now I decline again.

JUDITH. Inevitably.

LVOV. Decline, yes. And I want to see it.

JUDITH. What for?

LVOV. Witness it.

JUDITH. What for?

LVOV. Autumnal —

JUDITH. What —

LVOV. Etcetera —

JUDITH. What! *(He winces. Hides his head.)* Fear talking.

LVOV. Fear, obviously.

JUDITH. Lvov —

LVOV. I shall never know what it is to bite a peach and lose a tooth —

JUDITH. Lvov —

LVOV. Or see the brown skin hanging off my knee caps —

JUDITH *(sarcastically)*. Terrible deprivation —

LVOV. **I am entitled to that also.** *(Pause.)*

JUDITH. Are you? *(She gets up.)* Are you entitled to the mundane satisfactions of the common life?

LVOV. Yes!

JUDITH. You spit on common life.

LVOV. Yes!

JUDITH. Spit on it.

LVOV. All right, I spit! *(Pause.)* For one weary moment, I longed for friendship, simple, open-handed friendship . . .

JUDITH. The charismatic have no friends . . *(Pause.)*

LVOV. Judith, how you force greatness on me . . . and I would love to swerve . . . be kind — *(He reaches out.)*

JUDITH. Kindness!

**Murdered word.**
*(His hand drops. Pause.)* Die tonight, or I shall . . . sicken . . . do you understand me? Sicken. *(Pause.)*

LVOV. Yes. *(Pause.)* They will kill me. You must orchestrate it.

JUDITH. Yes.

LVOV. But more.

JUDITH. More?

LVOV. More, yes.

JUDITH. What more?

LVOV *(triumphantly).* **Ha! You are greater than me and you cannot imagine!**

JUDITH. What more?

LVOV. **She is greater and she cannot think!**

JUDITH. What? What more?

LVOV. Lvov! Lvov! The Great Imaginer! Lvov *(The cloud of laughter roars overhead.)*

CHORUS. Lvov was born the son of a bricklayer and his first language was
**Dialect**
Lvov looked at his father's house and experienced
**Disgust**
He stood on the railway station looking
**Ashamed**

LVOV. What's knowlege! It is prejudice grinding on the conscience . . .

CHORUS. And when the train came he climbed always into the compartment reserved for
**Women**

MARYA *(pause).* It rains on all the graves, so what? It rains on all the widows, so what? And the ill-fucked women, it rains on them. Lvov, I only liked you because you were not kind. You were not considerate, or gentle. You had immaculate manners but without charity. How I liked that! How I responded to that! You were not casual, nor carefree, keeping yourself at a cold distance, and touching no one. How I liked that! You did not tell me I was gifted. You never praised my poetry. How I liked that! How I responded! You never told me we could live at peace. Or apologized for acts that had no justification — *(She opens her blouse.)* Goodbye you male scum! *(She laughs.)*

LVOV *(to* JUDITH*).* When I am dead — when —

CHORUS. **Lvov**
**They're hungry**
**And they want their supper**

*Cloud of laughter*

LVOV. If I wish to live forever, I have to die.

CHORUS. **Feed them!**

LVOV. But more than die . . . they must consume me . . . *(Pause.* JUDITH *sways.)*

JUDITH. Why —

LVOV. **To live in the memory.** *(Pause.)*

JUDITH. Yes . . . it's perfectly true . . . I have no imagination . . . I am cleverer than you but with no imagination **how dare you**. Come up with such a **how could you inflict such**

LVOV. Do you think I'd die like anybody else? *(Pause.)*

JUDITH. And if we don't? If we revolt? If we say **enough manipulation from beyond the grave**? If we just chuck you on the tip? Another bit of old Europe? **Another corpse, what!**

LVOV. Obviously I place great faith in you.

JUDITH. Liar. Faith! You liar.

LVOV. You'll do it.

JUDITH. Why?

LVOV. Because you will want it finished. You will not settle for anything less. It's the investment the servant makes in servitude. *(Pause.)*

JUDITH. Kiss me.
    Kiss me.

*He kisses her cheek. The sound of desolation.*

### THE SEVENTH PARABLE
**The Authentic Madness of a Redundant Class**

McNOY *enters.*

McNOY. McStain is dead.
    McStain
    McStain.
    How he —
    His awful —
    Unforgettable McStain.
    The way he!
    And that habit of!
    Indelible McStain?
    *(Pause.)*With two our role is impossible to play. With two, no bell can be unslung. The officer who gave the order knew the necessity for three pairs of hands. The officer who is buried in the village square knew the subject. How well he knew! Which is rare among the givers of instructions. And now McStain is dead! Already McStain is fading. Indelible McStain! *(*MACATTLEE *enters.)*

MACATTLEE. I buried McStain. And burying him, I interred all memory. Who was McStain?

McNOY. I couldn't help, I was too moved.

MACATTLEE. No, I like digging. I like to dig alone. *(Pause.)*

McNOY. And now we.
    And so we.
    Where does that leave.

*Pause. They instantaneously engage in a cruel and relentless fight, pushing each other this way and that.* IVORY *appears. They cease, exhausted.*

IVORY. Who was McStain?
> I passed his grave in the Avenue of Poplars. *(The* MACS *look bewildered.)*
> I saw his crossed sticks on my return from the Knot Garden. *(Pause.)* I was
> coming from the Temple of the Four Winds when I saw —
> Please do not piss yourself laughing I am sorry you are sweating embarass-
> ment at every pore but I lived and loved here
> **Of course the landscape's different**
> *(Pause.)* The hamper spilled and her shoe came off, the label still inside. **How
> clean she was, oh, clean.** A shallow laugh however. Adorable shallowness. And
> I talked volubly. I, educated and in possession of three thousand books. **There!**
> *(He points to a barren spot.)* No one came near. The walls of the estate were
> higher than two men.

McNOY. I saw a wall . . .

IVORY. That was the wall —

McNOY. I saw a fragment of a wall —

IVORY. That was the wall. *(Pause.* McNOY *and* MacATTLEE, *by mute agree-*
> *ment, get up to leave.)*
> Pity the man who has no wall.
> Pity his limitless choice of.

*The* MACS *are about to walk away when bells are heard. They stop, by
instinct. Pause.*

IVORY *(darkly).* Shall I become McStain? *(They look at him.)*

McNOY. How could his way of —
> His habit of —

IVORY. I shall become McStain —

McNOY. His old trick of —

IVORY. I am McStain. *(Pause.* McNOY *looks at him.)*

McNOY. You are nothing like what I recall McStain to —

IVORY. I am sufficiently McStain to be McStain. Later I will be all that he con-
> sisted of. *(They are afraid of him. The Bells continue faintly.)* This is the way.
> *(He starts off. Stops.)*

MacATTLEE *(cunningly).* The wall. *(He winks at* McNOY.*)* Unfortunately the
> wall . . .

IVORY *(taking it from his pocket).* I have the key. *(He smiles.)* When she came,
> laughing shallowly, I locked the gate behind her, and as we tussled on the lawn
> the key fell out of my pocket. I looked all day for the key. Then the war came,
> passing and repassing. Today I found the key, flung up by the gravedigger.
> *(Pause.)*

McNOY. Well, then . . . *(They shrug.)*

MacATTLEE. McStain carried the ropes. *(He tosses a coil.)* And me the ham-
> mer. *(They set off.)*

IVORY. Already, I feel his nimbleness!

### *END OF THE SEVENTH PARABLE*

*The sleeping guests stir.*

ANNA *(to* LVOV*).* They talked about you! They said — I did too — what has made Lvov like this? They were — I was too — full of criticism and called you, for example — a sham. And said — me too — we were taken in by Lvov, who is a sham. Are you a sham, Lvov?

LVOV. Yes. Wake them up now. Kick them with your whore's heels. Drive them out their kip you frilled object.

ANNA. Lvov —

LVOV. You orphan of a bitch and a thin lout.

ANNA. You want me to hate you and all I feel is love! I was so angry with you and now I understand your loneliness, your —

GISELA. We talked.

ANNA. We hated you and then —

GISELA. We talked and we decided —

ANNA. We decided —

GISELA. The cruelty you did me no man could do were he not himself in **awful agony**. I saw how shallow my anger was. Nothing is lost of my terrible bond with you. Only more so. It is bound in nakedness and pain now, too . . .*(He stares at her.)*

ANNA. That's what I wanted to say! You said it beautifully! *(She hugs* GISELA.*)*

LVOV. But you must murder me. *(Pause. He looks around them.)*

SLOMAN. I have seen through you twice. The first time, I saw through your message. Second, I saw not only was your message failing, but that your provocations were an attempt to save your message. The message must die, and be seen to die. You must not be permitted to obscure the collapse of your teaching by a flamboyant death. *(Pause.)*

APOLLO. We said, Lvov is rude today, and sullen. Today we like him less that ever. But hate him? *(Pause.)*

LVOV. Listen.

I am the supper.

SLOMAN *(triumphantly).* You see! You see!

LVOV. If you don't hate me enough, love me enough!

SLOMAN. You see!

LVOV. **I am the supper!** *(A train passes, fast.)*

ELLA. The war is over! Now it'll be hell! *(Its lights and sound fade.)*

IVORY. I ate a woman once, who came to picnic on the terrace. It's not impossible. She sat in a cloud of finery and all the time the ribbons on her hat went twitter, twitter. How perfect she was clothed, and how perfect unclothed. How perfect her skin, and how perfect her inside. Her exterior, and her interior . . .

LVOV. I surrounded myself with murderers. Not knowing this. But what is accidental? I drew you all to me not planning this but who is better? **Help me I am capable of such cowardice.** I could so easily run in the dark crying love and love and kiss the wheels of filthy wagons, **hold me down, then!** *(He kneels. They are still.)*

JUDITH. And the bones will be relics. And sterile men will plead upon them, make me fecund!

SLOMAN. Anyone who goes near him, I will stab. *(He takes his carving knife.)*

IVORY. But we are so hungry, aren't we? So very hungry.

SLOMAN. Anyone, I'll stab! *(Pause.)*

JUDITH. Sloman, who fears the immortality of one man . . .

SLOMAN. No one to help his vanity to flourish. *(Pause.)* **Can't you see it's a trick!**
*(Pause.)*

ELLA. Of course it's a trick. Don't you want to be tricked? Oh, don't you ever
long to be properly tricked? *(Pause. SLOMAN looks at JUDITH in horror.)*

JUDITH. We have to kill Lvov, because he is ceasing to be Lvov.

SLOMAN. Yes . . .! Rejoice! Under the ballgown, the scab! And the rat on the
wedding cake! Rejoice!

ELLA. I will kill him rather than hear him utter a trivial thing. Me, Ella, alone.

SLOMAN. **What are you, a slave?**
*(LVOV bursts out laughing, ceases.)*
**What are you?** *(He looks around them.)*

FORJACKS. When Lvov is dead, I shall be the archivist, does everyone agree
with that? I am the scholar, so it's obvious I. *(Pause.)*

DORA. It's true, in every sense, that Lvov is no longer necessary to Lvov. It's even
possible, Lvov is an impediment to Lvov, and to our — adoration of him. I
think now, we own Lvov, and Lvov is in danger of becoming an embarrassment
. . . — And I speak as one who loves him —

ANNA. You don't need to say that —

DORA. I don't need to say that, no —

APOLLO *(walking forward to LVOV)*. Climb on my back. *(Pause.)*

LVOV. To gallop off? To break out of encirclement?
**Some do! Some have!**

SUSANNAH. I killed my husband and buried him in the marsh. In three parts.
I rowed him. How my arse ached, and how happy I was! And Lvov praised
me. He sang me a song . . .

APOLLO. Climb on my back. Die on my back.

SUSANNAH. What a song. The words came automatically to him . . .!

MARYA. Lvov never sang.

SUSANNAH. He did sing. He sang that once.

MARYA. Lvov abhorred all singing. *(LVOV lets out a cry.)*

APOLLO. Many men died on my back. I carried them, like a mule. So much
carrying, and the telling of comforting anecdotes. And at the dressing station, putting them down, found them unworthy of the effort. Found them,
ungratefully, expired. Climb on. *(LVOV utters a horror.)* Oh, yes, the offer's
serious.

ANNA. To die among friends. To die at the hands of friends, is, surely, the mark
of the divine . . . *(APOLLO crouches.)*

SLOMAN. I insist on describing the nature of this madness, I insist on exposing
this irrationality, I will reveal to you notwithstanding your intoxication the
appalling fraud which is being perpetrated!

LVOV. Oh, I a little baby! Oh, I a little thing, mother! *(APOLLO locks arms in
LVOV's and hoists him on his back.)* Judith!

ANNA. He calls Judith. I was his love but he calls Judith . . .!

LVOV *(voluble, in a panic)*. I tell a story of a boy a lonely boy who never smiled
except to please and never laughed except to hide from those already

laughing — **Judith!** *(JUDITH takes the knife from* SLOMAN, *who is watching, transfixed.)* **JUD—ITH!** *(She approaches him.)* It's not what I want! **It's not what I want!** *(She thrusts the blade with determination.)*

ANNA. Me! Me! *(She takes the blade from* LVOV's *body and plunges it in.)*

CHORUS. **We express the common man's**
**The man in the street's objection to**

LVOV. Changed my mind . . .!

CHORUS. **The arrogance of**
**And the special pleading** *(*DORA *goes up, and stabs* LVOV.*)*

DORA. Oh, that, how unconvincing! *(She goes to* LVOV *again.)* How tentative and unconvincing! *(She stabs again.)*

CHORUS. **We don't accept the innocence of**
**We will not tolerate the mocking of**
**our**
*(As* MARYA *stabs* LVOV.*)*
**Loneliness**

JUDITH. Lvov? Is the light going?
They say the light goes, is the light going?

MARYA. I do it!

DORA. **We want**
**We want**
**A room with a view**

APOLLO *(as others stab)*. I feel him going . . .

JUDITH. He can't be, he promised to describe it, whisper me, Lvov — *(She goes near to him.)* Whisper! *(They begin, in an intoxicated way, to hop up and down.)*

CHORUS. **We want**
**We want**
**Sex in a bedroom**

ARNOLD *(stabbing)*. You are not better than me! No one is better than me!

CHORUS. **We want to be ashamed**
**We want**
**We want to be ashamed**
**We want**

*The door flies open, the crash acting like a bell in a boxing ring. The* MURDERERS *are still, hands in their mouths. Pause.*

FARMER. Is that Lvov?
Obviously, Lvov. . .
He's killed himself in order not to speak to me. *(He takes a grubby book from his pocket, flings it at the wall.)*
Message of Lvov . . .

SLOMAN. The master's dead.
Eat the master.
The master's dead.
You'll never be free now. *(He looks at the* FARMER, *who has a penknife out.)*
What are you doing?

FARMER *(sawing at* LVOV*)*. Taking a finger, he won't need —

SLOMAN. **What are you doing!**
FARMER. Taking a —
SLOMAN. **What for!**
FARMER *(sawing).* I can show this.
FORJACKS. Show it?
FARMER. Show it, yes — *(He waves the knife.)*
   **Get away.**
   I got nothing from Lvov, so Lvov can serve me now. There are places where
   they revere him. *(He cuts it off.)*
   **Finger of Lvov! Authentic!**
   Don't stand in my way, I have a living to make. *(He goes out.)*
APOLLO. I shall put him down, now. Put him on what, though? Someone speak
   . . . *(They are silent.)* Or should I carry him my whole life? Is that what you
   want? Through wind and sun? I could do.
ELLA. We have to save Lvov. From the Lvovites.
SLOMAN. You see! Once you begin! You see! He governs you!
DORA. I found the stabbing easy. I don't think stabbing him was any sacrifice.
   Did you?
IVORY. Easy.
DORA. Easy, yes.
SLOMAN *(to the dead* LVOV*).* **Manipulator!**
GISELA. His ordeal is over. Ours now. Or they will carry him to every corner
   of the earth.
SLOMAN *(with a sickly laugh).* I really think, I really, really think —
JUDITH. Knife, then, and basin . . .
SLOMAN. **There is no controlling you.** *(He shudders, then with decision.)* I'll
   eat Lvov. I will partake.
IVORY. Thank you.
SLOMAN. I will because this scheme of his is nothing but a plot to bind you
   in mystification. I will call **the corpses bluff**. Butcher! I will swallow and be
   not less but a greater cynic. Butcher! *(He drags the knife from* LVOV's *body.*
   *He stands, holding it, defiant. The wind of desolation.)*


### THE EIGHTH PARABLE
### *The Complex Origins of Domesticity*


McNOY *and* McATLEE *are carrying* IVORY *in a chair. They stop. The cloud
of laughter passes.*


McNOY. Who is cheering?
MacATTLEE. I've heard cheering before, but this is disembodied.
IVORY. It is the irrepressible expression of solidarity which has become detach-
   ed from humanity and drifts over the landscape. Why have you stopped? Did
   you think it was for you? *(*McNOY *shrugs.)*
MacATTLEE. He thought —
McNOY. No, no —

IVORY. He thought it was for him! *(*McNOY *shakes his head.)*
He thought it was gratitude! *(*McNOY *shakes his head.)*
Yes!
He still yearns for appreciation! *(He smiles.* MacATTLEE *shakes his head with amusement. A* WOMAN *appears, holding a pair of trousers.)*

SEAMTRESS *(to* IVORY*)*. Aren't you McStain?

IVORY. I am, I think, entirely McStain.

SEAMSTRESS. I ask because I have been darning his trousers. *(She holds them out.)* He paid in advance, so I knew he must come back.

IVORY. He has. As you say, it was inevitable. *(He reaches for them.)*

MacATTLEE. She is lying, despite her wonderful breasts. We never came this way before.

SEAMSTRESS. I never forget a face.

MacATTLEE. She is looking for a husband and this is a trick to demonstrate her needlework. Don't believe it, McStain.

IVORY. But I can see these are a perfect fit.

MacATTLEE. You are fascinated, and that has nothing to do with the truth or otherwise of what she says. *(To the* SEAMSTRESS*.)* If you are a needlewoman, show us other trousers. *(She pulls out other pairs.)* You see! She is a consummate liar!

IVORY. Put the chair down. I want to examine her.

MacATTLEE. No! You are as smitten as the crew of Odysseus in the locality of sirens. Don't put him down, or we shall be a bellman short.

SEAMSTRESS. You're quite right. I am looking for a husband and I've never heard of McStain.

MacATTLEE. You see! This is what we have to guard against! And her breasts are forever pleading their case. Look away, McNoy . . .

IVORY *(persisting)*. I am a landowner. Do you find me attractive?

SEAMSTRESS. From my first glance.

McNOY. It's all up with us . . .

IVORY *(hopping down)*. This is the parting of the ways.

SEAMSTRESS *(to* IVORY*)*. When I look at you I feel no shyness. We shall join together, and I will see clouds over your shoulder, and you will see grass under my head.

MacATTLEE. McStain, I have to warn you, is a murderer and a cannibal.

SEAMSTRESS. Let him murder me. He is beautiful and a landowner. I would be happy to be murdered by such a man.

MacATTLEE. How she simpers! And what is that on her mouth? It's the stain of some wild berry which in my opinion utterly fails to enhance her appearance. Come on, McStain, the world is full of belfries!

IVORY *(eyes on the* SEAMSTRESS*)*. Leave the chair. It is the beginning of our home.

MacATTLEE. It is the beginning of delusion.

IVORY *(taking down the chair)*. Sit, sit my love . . . *(As she does so,* McNOY *strikes a fatal blow on* IVORY's *head. He falls.)*

McNOY. I'm sorry! I'm sorry! I'm sorry!

MacATTLEE. We kill nobody!

McNOY *(hopping about in horror)*. I'm so sorry! I'm so sorry!

MACATTLEE *(beside* IVORY*)*. Oh, McStain, what could she have given you?
  *(They all look at the dead figure of* IVORY. *The* SEAMSTRESS *turns to go,
  then stops. She looks at the trousers she is holding.)*
SEAMSTRESS. Is one of you McNoy. . . ?

### END OF THE EIGHTH PARABLE


*The* DISCIPLES *are distributed over the stage. They are stooping on all
fours, or sitting with their knees drawn up, still and silent as in a tableau. An
appalling silence. A single sound. Silence.*

ARNOLD. We did it and — *(A cacophony as everyone launches into speech.)*
  Shut up! *(Silence, long, still.)*
  And then — *(Cacophony breaks out again.)*
MARYA. **Shut up!** *(Silence, long, still. At last* SLOMAN *rises to his feet.)*
SLOMAN. Hold hands.
  We mustn't part.
  Hold hands. *(He extends his hands. No one moves. He cries out in despair.)*
  **Hold hands!**

*Silence. The door opens. The* FIRST OFFICER *enters. He wears a sash.*

OFFICER. The war has ended and I have come to claim Lvov. *(No one moves.)*
  To settle with those whose statements were not clear. The ones who failed to
  simplify. And the wearers of glasses. *(Pause.)* Are you hiding Lvov? *(Pause.)*
  Some of you will be hanged. And the women given medicines. Where is Lvov?
JUDITH. Gone. *(Pause. He looks at them, turns to go.)*
APOLLO. Was it hard out there?
OFFICER. Hard? You couldn't call it hard. And yet, if I say it was not hard,
  you will think it was easy, so I don't know what to say. Accuracy is impossi-
  ble. We abandoned accuracy in the first few days. Without accuracy, things
  become tolerable . . . *(Pause.)* Report, if Lvov shows up.
JUDITH. He won't.
OFFICER. What makes you certain? *(Pause.)* The certainty of you people! When
  everything shows that nothing is certain. *(He turns to go, treads on something.
  He disdains to look down.)* What is that?
JUDITH. Spectacles.
OFFICER. He is here, then. He could not travel without spectacles. *(Pause.)*
SLOMAN. Yes.
  He's here. *(The cloud of laughter passes.)*
ANNA. He wanted praise, but not from us. He thirsted for applause, but the
  applause of the select.
JUDITH. Who this select was, he never said. *(The cloud again.)*
OFFICER. Show me Lvov.
SLOMAN. **Hold hands!** *(They hold hands. The* OFFICER *is poised, wary. Pause.
  Voices are heard, singing badly. The* TWO MACS *enter.)*

### THE SONG

THE MACS. How skilful we have been
  To make sure we were seen
  **Reluctant**
  How tactful we behaved
  At the palace or the cave
  **Abject**
  And playing cards we choose
  Invariably to lose
  **Inoffensive**
  We took the long way round but we arrived
  And if the pub has disappeared
  Where we watched girls slyly
  In the grip of the sexually proud
  **Well**
  And if the bed's been commandeered
  Where we kipped late in the morning
  And the mothers are all lying in their shrouds
  **Well**
  The thieves have shit my sheets
  And my one and only suit
  Is on the back of a dog that's going mental
  But we arrived
  **And if we killed it was purely accidental**

OFFICER *(seizing the opportunity)*. **Rope them!** *(*THE MACS *are momentarily dumbfounded.)* **Rope them!** *(Their instinct returns.* McNOY *casts off the bell ropes and they run around the* DISCIPLES, *pulling them into a tight noose. They knot the ropes. Pause. The sound of a distant celebration.* THE MACS *sit on the floor and smoke. The* OFFICER *drifts towards the sound.)*

SUSSANAH. He had the flavour of —

ALL. **Don't mention it!**

SUSANNAH. He had the texture of —

ALL. **Don't dare describe it!** *(Pause. The knot of* DISCIPLES *drifts, first one way, then another. The cloud passes overhead.)*